D1544672

THE CALIFORNIA GOLD RUSH

MILESTONES
IN
AMERICAN HISTORY

MILESTONES
IN
AMERICAN HISTORY

THE CALIFORNIA
GOLD RUSH

TRANSFORMING THE AMERICAN WEST

LIZ SONNEBORN

CHELSEA HOUSE
PUBLISHERS
An imprint of Infobase Publishing

The California Gold Rush

Copyright © 2009 by Infobase Publishing

Chelsea House
An imprint of Infobase Publishing
132 West 31st Street
New York NY 10001

Library of Congress Cataloging-in-Publication Data

Sonneborn, Liz.
  The California gold rush : transforming the American West / by Liz Sonneborn.
     p. cm. — (Milestones in American history)
  Includes bibliographical references and index.
  ISBN 978-1-60413-051-5 (hardcover)
  1. California—Gold discoveries—Juvenile literature. 2. California—History—
1846–1850—Juvenile literature. 3. Gold mines and mining—California—History—
19th century—Juvenile literature. I. Title. II. Series.
  F865.S76 2008
  978'.02—dc22   2008024151

Series design by Erik Lindstrom
Cover design by Ben Peterson

Printed in the United States of America

Bang NMSG 10 9 8 7 6 5 4 3 2 1

This book is printed on acid-free paper.

All links and Web addresses were checked and verified to be correct at the time of publication. Because of the dynamic nature of the Web, some addresses and links may have changed since publication and may no longer be valid.

CONTENTS

"Gold from the American River!"

On December 18, 1847, Azariah Smith, then 19 years old, confided his sorrows to his diary. Against his wishes, he was stuck in the unfamiliar land of California, hundreds of miles away from his beloved parents and sisters. He wrote, "Home keeps running in my mind, and I feel somewhat lonesume especially Sundays, but my heart leaps with the expection of getting home in the spring, and again it sometimes shrinks for fear that I will fail for want of means, but I keep up as good courage as I can."[1]

Smith arrived in California in 1846 as part of the Mormon Battalion. The battalion was formed by Brigham Young, leader of the Mormon Church (also called the Church of Latter-day Saints), at the request of the U.S. government to help fight a war with Mexico. Smith was an unenthusiastic soldier but a loyal Mormon. When Young asked for volunteers, he dutifully signed up.

During the war, the Mormon Battalion was sent to California to act as part of an occupying American force in this Mexican territory. Smith was stationed near San Diego when his year of military service came to an end on July 20, 1847. He desperately wanted to return to his family, but a letter from the Mormons' leaders instructed the battalion's veterans to stay in California until the following spring and to find paying work. Once again, Smith did as he was told. He and his comrades headed north to the little town of San Francisco to find jobs.

AT SUTTER'S MILL

Near the town, eight years earlier, a Swiss man named Johann Sutter had built a compound at the confluence of the American and Sacramento rivers. He grandly called it New Helvetia (meaning New Switzerland). Nearly everyone else referred to it simply as Sutter's Fort. It was an important center for trade in the region.

Sutter offered a job to any of the Mormons who wanted one. With three other battalion veterans, Smith went to work on a sawmill on the American River about 40 miles from Sutter's Fort. Their work was overseen by James Marshall, Sutter's business partner in the mill. The job was physically demanding, especially when the winter ushered in the rainy season. Working hard day after day, often in pouring rain, left the once-hardy 19-year-old weak and sickly. During one bout of fever, Smith began to fear that he would not survive. He wrote, "I felt bad the thought running in my mind that likely I [would] never see home again which was a perfect torment to my mind."[2] As bad as the work was, his homesickness was even worse.

Smith and his coworkers also had more petty concerns. Sutter supplied them with shelter and food, but both left much to be desired. Their cabin lacked ventilation and would fill up with smoke if they lit a fire during cool winter nights. They

Built near the meeting point of the American and Sacramento rivers, Sutter's Fort was an important trading center in the area.

were furious with their cook who, as Smith noted, only gave them "Beaf, and Bread," and kept the best foodstuffs—"the pumpkin &c"[3]—for herself and her family.

A DISCOVERY ON THE AMERICAN RIVER

In his diary entry for January 30, 1848, Smith began with the big news of the week. The Mormons had confronted Marshall with their complaints. He let them build their own house and got rid of the "brawling, partial"[4] cook.

Only after his enthusiastic recounting of these victories did Smith note that something else had happened about a week earlier: "This week Mon. 24th Mr. Marshall found some pieces of (as we all suppose) Gold, and he has gone to the Fort, for the Purpose of finding out. It is found in the raceway in small pieces; some have been found that would [be worth] five dollars."[5]

To Smith, the gold find seemed barely worth a mention in his journal. Marshall was much more enthusiastic about his discovery. He later remembered the morning of January 24, when he spied in the icy water of the American River one flake of shiny metal, then another, then another. According to Marshall, "It made my heart thump, for I was certain it was gold."[6]

When Marshall arrived at the fort, Sutter took him to the office and locked the door. There, the two examined the metal specimens Marshall had found. After consulting the *Encyclopedia Americana* about the properties of pure gold, they ran a series of tests. Each one confirmed that Marshall was right. He had indeed found gold.

THE NEWS SPREADS

Sutter told Marshall to keep the news to himself. At that point, the only other people who knew about the gold were the Mormons working on the mill, so Marshall made a deal with them. As Smith wrote, "Mr. Marshall grants us the privelege of picking up Gold odd spells and Sundays, and I have gathered up considerable."[7] For this privilege, Marshall took half of whatever gold the Mormons could poke out of the ground with their fingers or their pocketknives.

For Smith, the gold he found was something of a relief. All winter long he had worried about taking time from work because of illness. He was afraid that his pay would not be enough to buy the necessary provisions for the trip to the Mormon settlement at Salt Lake in the spring. With the gold he was pocketing, though, Smith finally was sure to have the money he needed to return to his family.

Even so, Smith was not entirely comfortable with gold hunting. To the deeply religious young man, it seemed vaguely immoral. Only half jokingly, he wrote in his diary, "Today I picked up a little more of the root of all evil."[8]

GOLD FEVER!

Sutter did not share Smith's mixed feelings about the gold. In fact, as the Mormons labored away, Sutter made a move to ensure that he could claim all of the gold for himself: He gave Indians in the area some shirts, shoes, and other American goods in exchange for a three-year lease of the land surrounding the mill. Then he sent a messenger with the agreement to the city of Monterey. Sutter wanted Richard Mason, the new American governor of California stationed there, to give it his official approval. Sutter's plan backfired. Not only did Mason refuse to approve the lease, but Sutter's messenger blabbed about the gold find to anyone who would listen. The word was out.

Even so, most people in California were skeptical. Six years earlier, they had heard of a major gold strike in Los Angeles. People rushed there, eager to strike it rich, only to find that the claims were wildly exaggerated. What the doubters needed was real proof of the gold strike. On May 12, a merchant named Sam Brannan gave them just that. Brannan had established a store that sold supplies for miners. Perhaps to drum up business, he walked through the muddy streets of San Francisco holding up a bottle full of gold flakes while shouting, "Gold! Gold! Gold from the American River!"[9] Within days, Brannan's stunt had set off a rush to the gold fields: The town's newspaper reported about "a terrible visitant we have had of late, a FEVER which has well nigh depopulated our town, a town hard pressing upon a thousand souls. And this is the GOLD FEVER."[10]

A STRIKE ON MORMON ISLAND

Just as Brannan was shaking up San Francisco, Azariah Smith and a few friends were camped out on a large sandbar on the American River. The sandbar was nicknamed Mormon Island, because two Mormons were the first to discover new gold there. Smith mined at Mormon Island for 12 days with spectacular results. As he wrote in his journal, "While there we had very good luck; I got there something near three hundred dollars, which makes me in all some upwards of four hundred dollars. The most I made in a day was sixty five dollars."[11] At the time, a farmhand might earn one dollar for a long day of

News of the gold discovery at Sutter's Fort spread to the East and sparked a massive migration of people seeking their fortune. Many families in the United States hitched up their wagons and traveled west, hoping to get their share of the precious mineral.

hard labor. Understandably, Smith was quite impressed by his $65 payday.

So was everyone else who got wind of what was going on at Mormon Island. Smith wrote, "Before we came away, men, women, and children, from the [San Francisco] Bay and other places in California, were flocking to the gold mine, by the dozens, and by wagon loads."[12]

Just as gold seekers were pouring into the area, Smith was preparing to leave. In late June 1848, he got his pay from Sutter and joined a wagon train bound for Salt Lake. He found his family and settled in the town of Manti in Utah.

THE RUSH BEGINS

For Azariah Smith, one of the few eyewitnesses to the discovery of gold in California, the Gold Rush had come to an end. The homesick 19-year-old seemed to have had no trouble giving up dreams of gold in order to be reunited with his family. In the months and years to come, however, Smith's ability to walk away from easy riches proved to be a rare quality. For hundreds of thousands of Americans, the lure of free gold, just waiting to be plucked from the ground, was too intoxicating to ignore.

The men, women, and children Smith saw flooding onto Mormon Island were just the start. Each week that passed, new gold fields were found, drawing in more and more treasure seekers. Over the next decade, hundreds of thousands of miners arrived in California. The influx would constitute the greatest migration in the history of the United States, and Americans were not the only people who caught gold fever. Men from all corners of the globe came to try their luck, making San Francisco the most multicultural society in the world for a time.

For individuals caught up in the Gold Rush, the era would always be remembered as a pivotal time in their lives. Some miners looked back on it as their greatest adventure; others, as their biggest mistake. The women and children they left behind recalled their struggles and loneliness, celebrating the ways they met the challenges and bemoaning the ways they could not.

The Gold Rush affected not only the people directly involved in it; it altered American life then and forever after. The Gold Rush reshaped the United States by drastically accelerating immigration to the West. It transformed American society, as many citizens embraced a new-found independence they discovered in California. Perhaps most important, it remolded the American character, turning a country of settled farmers into a nation of forward-thinking risk takers. Introducing new ideas about work and wealth, luck and greed, and success and failure, the Gold Rush changed the way Americans looked at their lives, their livelihoods, and, most of all, themselves.

A Land of Plenty

It is known that to the right of the Indies there exists an island called California very near the terrestrial paradise. . . . [I]n all the island there was no metal except gold."[1]

These words were written in 1510, 338 years before gold was actually discovered in California. The California described in the passage was not the place we know by that name today; it was a fantasy from the imagination of a Spanish novelist who wrote of a golden land ruled by a fictional warrior-queen named Calafia. The story of Calafia's realm was popular with the Spanish, who would find real lands filled with gold in the Americas shortly thereafter.

In 1521, Hernán Cortés conquered the Aztecs of present-day Mexico, and in 1532, Francisco Pizarro overwhelmed the Incas of what is now Peru. The Spanish conquistadores plundered the Aztec and Inca empires, taking back to Spain an astounding amount of gold, precious stones, and other treasures. All of these riches left the Spanish crown hungry for more, and thus Spain's royals funded more expeditions to search for other wealthy empires that they could exploit. In 1542, they sponsored an exploration headed by Portuguese explorer Juan Rodríguez Cabrillo. Cabrillo headed north from Mexico up the coast of present-day California. The lands he explored and claimed became known as California, after Queen Calafia's kingdom. Despite the name, however, Cabrillo found no gold there. All he discovered were Indian peoples who appeared to have none of the riches the Spanish were looking for. Based on Cabrillo's disappointing report, the Spanish largely ignored the area for more than 200 years.

CALIFORNIA'S NATIVES

Cabrillo may not have been impressed by the wealth of the natives of California, but they were actually among the most prosperous of all Indian peoples in North America. It was easy to thrive in their environment: The climate was generally mild, and their lands provided them with a wide variety of food sources. Depending on where they lived, the Indians of California could fish, hunt, collect shellfish, and gather nuts, fruits, berries, seeds, and roots. They had so many ways to get food that they did not even bother to learn how to grow crops.

With their abundant surroundings, California's Indian population became very large. By the mid-eighteenth century, the area was home to more than 300,000 people, making it the most densely populated region anywhere in North America north of present-day Mexico.

California's plentiful environment also allowed its Indians to get all the necessities of life without much effort. As a result, they did not need to travel and trade as much as other Indian peoples did. They generally lived in small, isolated tribal groups that had little, if any, contact with one another.

THE MISSION SYSTEM

The Spanish renewed their interest in California in the eighteenth century when they learned that Russians were hunting off the coast of present-day Alaska. The Spanish feared that the Russians might start to move south and challenge the Spanish claim to California, and the best way to protect their claim was to populate the region with Spaniards. Few Spaniards wanted to live in faraway California, however, even when they were offered large plots of free land. The Spanish government therefore came up with a new plan: the mission system.

Under this system, Catholic priests and soldiers ventured to California, where they constructed buildings and planted gardens in various areas. They then tried to lure nearby Indian people to live at these crude settlements. These Indians would then become a labor force that would expand the missions. At the same time, the priests would convert the Indians to Christianity and teach them Spanish ways. The first mission was built at San Diego in 1769. By 1823, there were 20 other missions in operation.

For Indians, life at the missions was brutal and often short. The priests used beatings or imprisonment to control the Indian populations, and, even worse, the Spanish introduced Indians to European diseases such as measles and smallpox, to which they had no immunity. Epidemics spread quickly, sometimes killing as many 90 percent of the Indians in a mission. Even Indians who had never seen a Spaniard were infected by mission Indians who returned to their villages after being exposed.

Everyone at the missions suffered from the neglect of the Spanish government. Often, promised supplies never arrived, so the Spaniards at the missions eventually came to rely on another source for the goods they needed but could not produce themselves.

Beginning in 1796, American trading ships bound for China began to stop at California's ports. The Spaniards offered the traders otter pelts and cattle hides, which the traders could

Known as the "King of Missions," San Luis Rey de Francia *(above)* was the second mission to be built in the San Diego area. American Indians who stayed at these missions were used as labor, and many contracted European diseases, which resulted in a dramatic decrease of the native population.

resell in China at a steep markup. In return, the traders gave the Spaniards cotton, blankets, shoes, fishhooks, and other manufactured items. The American traders also brought some exotic luxury items obtained through the China trade. It was not unusual for people at the missions to wear camel-hair shawls or eat off of porcelain plates.

CALIFORNIO RANCHERS

In 1821, the Spanish government in Mexico fell apart, and Mexico became an independent nation. The new government was highly unstable, however, with different factions constantly battling for power. Concentrating on their own struggles, Mexican officials paid no more attention to California than Spanish officials had. There was one aspect of California life that interested the leaders in Mexico City, however: They hungrily eyed the missions and the areas near them. To get their hands on these fertile, settled lands, which officially belonged to the Catholic Church, Mexican officials secularized the missions.

In theory, the Indians who lived and worked there were to take over for the exiting priests. Instead, Mexican officials gave themselves or their friends and relatives huge land grants, some as big as 700,000 acres. On these land grants, they established large ranches that were operated by forced Indian labor. Ranch owners lived a life of leisure, spending most of their time holding dances and celebrating holidays and weddings.

The Spaniards on these ranches, who became known as Californios, were also enthusiastic customers for American traders. They did not bother to establish their own industries. They preferred to rely on traders to bring them manufactured items. The ranch families also showed little interest in developing their communities. They did not establish any schools, newspapers, or hospitals, or even build roads. The ranchers were content to travel in primitive carts pulled by oxen along old dirt trails.

HEADING TO CALIFORNIA

American traders shared stories about the Californios with people back home. They came to hold these ranching families in contempt, particularly in New England, where most of the traders were from. Americans tended to view hard work as a moral obligation. In their eyes, the ranchers did not deserve their land because they were not making the most of it. In his famous book *Two Years Before the Mast*, Richard Dana wrote what many Americans were thinking: "In the hands of an enterprising people, what a country [California] might be."[2]

In the early 1840s, a few Americans decided to become those enterprising people of whom Dana had dreamed. For several years, a trickle of Americans had started to travel overland to settle on Oregon farmland. The route they took was called the Oregon Trail. In 1841, mountain man Jedediah Smith blazed an offshoot of the Oregon Trail that led into northern California. Traveling along the California Trail, about 6,000 Americans made their way there by 1846.

No one tried to stop them. The Mexican authorities did not have the power or will to keep them out, and the Californios did not mind the newcomers as long as they did not try to settle directly on the Californios' lands. California's Indians were in no position to object, even if they wanted to. By that time, disease and years of abuse had so weakened the Indians that they focused what energy they had left on avoiding confrontations rather than seeking them out.

MAKING CALIFORNIA AMERICAN

The Americans, mostly farming families, set about building a future in California. Among them was the enterprising Thomas Larkin. Settling in the capital of Monterey, he established a bakery, a flour mill, a blacksmith shop, and even a bowling alley.

The most ambitious newcomer, though, was Johann Sutter. A Swiss immigrant who had abandoned his wife and children to come to America, Sutter built a compound of buildings and businesses near the town of Yerba Buena (later renamed San Francisco). It became a gathering place where Americans could trade and socialize with one another. Like the Spanish priests and Mexican ranchers, Sutter relied on the labor of Indians, whom he treated like slaves. They tended his fields and orchards and kept his herds of cattle, horses, and sheep. Sutter, who made up impressive military titles for himself, kept his fort safe from intruders with a private army made up of Indians

Johann Sutter *(above)* traveled to America to avoid his creditors in Switzerland and made his way to California. Granted 50,000 acres of land by the Mexican governor in Monterey, Sutter built New Helvetia into a successful settlement and trading post.

who marched military drills wearing green and blue uniforms that Sutter bought from the Russians.

(continues on page 18)

JOHN C. FRÉMONT
(1813–1890)

Pathfinder of the West

One of the most important and colorful people in early California history was John C. Frémont. Born in Savannah, Georgia, in 1813, Frémont joined the U.S. Army Corps of Topographical Engineers in 1838. The corps was charged with surveying unmapped areas within the United States.

After several surveying expeditions, Frémont met and married Jessie Benton, daughter of Thomas Hart Benton, a Missouri senator who lent his support to additional western explorations led by Frémont. Frémont recorded his journeys in *A Report of the Exploring Expedition to Oregon and California* (1845), which he wrote in collaboration with his wife. A bestseller, the book introduced thousands of Americans in the East to the wonders of the West.

During the Mexican-American War, the ambitious Frémont headed for northern California. With about 100 Americans, he staged a revolt against Mexican rule without the approval of the U.S. Army. During the short-lived rebellion, Frémont followers waved a crude flag bearing an image of a bear. The event became known as the Bear Flag Rebellion.

Once California was secured under U.S. military occupation, Frémont made another rash power grab and declared himself governor. General Stephen Kearny challenged Frémont, leading to his arrest and court-martial. Recognizing that Frémont had become a popular American hero, President James Polk remitted the sentence, but Frémont nevertheless quit the army in disgust over the incident.

Col. JOHN C. FREMONT,
REPUBLICAN CANDIDATE FOR PRESIDENT OF THE UNITED STATES.

Explorer John C. Frémont was an extremely popular figure in the American West. He led a short-lived revolt against the Mexican officials in California in 1846. Ten years later, Frémont became the first Republican candidate for president, but he lost to his Democratic rival, James Buchanan.

Frémont's luck turned with the discovery of gold in California. He had previously purchased a large tract of land that just happened to be in the middle of the gold region. The gold there eventually made him extremely wealthy. Venturing into politics, he was elected to the Senate in 1849 and ran an unsuccessful campaign for the presidency in 1856.

Frémont went on to dabble in railroad deals, some of dubious legality. Late in life, he served as the governor of Arizona Territory. After retiring to California, he died during a visit to New York City in 1890.

(continued from page 15)

THE MEXICAN-AMERICAN WAR

Like the American settlers, officials in Washington, D.C., had taken note of the reports about California's rich and largely unsettled lands. Presidents Andrew Jackson and John Tyler both attempted to buy California from Mexico. President James K. Polk was even more driven to make California part of the United States.

After an unsuccessful attempt to purchase California, Polk's secretary of state asked Thomas Larkin to secretly discover how the Californians would feel about coming under American control. Larkin found that not only the Americans but also the Californios would welcome it. Everyone in northern California, it seemed, was tired of Mexico's neglect and eager to establish real government institutions in the region.

In the meantime, Polk sent American troops into an area in Texas that was then claimed by both the United States and Mexico. The president meant to provoke a war. He soon got his wish. After Mexican soldiers fired on the Americans, the United States declared war on Mexico on May 13, 1846.

Two months later, John Sloat, commodore of the U.S. fleet in the Pacific, arrived in Monterey. He took the California capital without a fight, and California found itself under American military occupation.

THE FUTURE OF CALIFORNIA

Californios to the north generally accepted the new state of affairs. Those to the south in the town of Los Angeles, however, rebelled against American rule in September 1846. An influx of U.S. soldiers put down the revolt and reclaimed the town in January 1847.

The actual fighting of the Mexican-American War in California had come to an end. Now the waiting began. Everyone was edgy, eager to hear how the war was going on other fronts, but they had no way to get news quickly. It was decades before the invention of the telephone. The telegraph had just been invented, but at that point no telegraph wires connected California to either the Mexican or the U.S. capitals.

As 1847 began, Californios and Americans in California were in limbo. They could assume that the Americans were winning the war, but they could not know for sure what that would mean for California. None of them could have guessed that another event would not only change everything about their lives but everything about California as well.

California in 1848

On February 2, 1848, nine days after the discovery of gold in California, the United States and Mexico signed the Treaty of Guadalupe Hidalgo. This treaty officially ended the Mexican-American War. In exchange for $15 million, defeated Mexico agreed to cede almost half of its lands to the United States. The ceded territory included parts or all of the present-day states of Nevada, Utah, Arizona, New Mexico, Colorado, Wyoming, and California.

Given the slow speed of communication, Californians did not learn of the treaty until August. In San Francisco, they celebrated with a display of fireworks and a parade through the streets. The revelers were happy and relieved to hear that California was now part of the United States, but it was far from the most important news they had received that year. By that time, everything in California was overshadowed by James Marshall's sighting of gold specks in the American River and the frenzy that followed.

"NOTHING BUT GOLD, GOLD, GOLD!"

By the summer of 1848, the gold rush was on. Even skeptical Californians had come to believe that the discovery was real after Sam Brannan walked through San Francisco waving his vial of gold for all to see. Entrepreneur Thomas Larkin wrote of the excitement: "We can hear of nothing but Gold, Gold, Gold! An ounce a day, two a day or three—everyone had the gold or yellow fever. . . . I think nine tenths of every store keep, mechanic or day laborer of this town [Monterey] and perhaps of San Francisco will leave for the Sacramento [River]."[1]

The fever also affected sailors on the trading ships that arrived in San Francisco's port. Hearing of the gold find, they left their ships in order to rush to the mines. San Francisco Bay was full of abandoned vessels. One man wrote that their high wooden masts made it look like a forest was growing out the water.

Richard B. Mason, the military governor of California, also remarked on the manpower shortage: "Laboring men at the mines can now earn in one day more than double a soldier's pay and allowances for a month, and even the pay of a lieutenant or captain cannot hire a servant. . . . Could any combination of affairs try a man's fidelity more than this?"[2] For Mason, the desertion of his soldiers posed a serious problem. He needed them to keep the peace in California, which still had no formal government, much less an organized police force.

His dwindling army also created a situation unique among gold rushes. In the past, government authorities inevitably demanded some, if not all, of the wealth generated by discoveries of precious minerals. In theory, the United States in 1848 was no different. The Land Ordinance of 1785 held that the federal government was entitled to one-third of any gold or other minerals found on land in the public domain.

In practice, however, Mason did not have the troops to enforce this or any law. He admitted as much in a report to Washington, D.C.: "Upon considering the large extent of the country, the character of the people engaged and the small, scattered force at my command, I resolved not to interfere but to permit all to work freely."[3] After Mason's decision, there was no going back. Any gold nugget a miner plucked from the ground would go directly into his pocket.

PICKS AND PANS

The miners' freedom to take whatever gold they could find, without buying a license or paying a tax, was only part of why so many men rushed to the California mines. Another attraction was the ease of mining there. The gold in California was known as "placer gold." Its loose flakes and nuggets were found stuck in the gravel and dirt of riverbeds. Picking up placer gold required far less work than extracting gold embedded in the rock faces.

In the early months of the rush, miners could do well working with the simplest of tools. Some had nothing more than a pick to stir the gravel and a knife to pick out any flakes they could spy, and a few used Indian baskets to sift through the dirt. Even something as commonplace as a woolen blanket could be a mining tool: Miners shoveled wet river dirt onto the blanket and allowed it dry in the sun. They then shook away the dirt, leaving the heavier gold particles clinging to the wool.

The mining tool of choice, however, quickly became the pan. Made from sheet iron, mining pans were round, with a diameter of about one foot. A pan had a flat bottom surrounded by gently sloping sides about four inches wide.

Panning for gold was a simple process: A miner filled the pan with dirt and then washed it in a river. The flow of the

#357. "We have It Rich." - Washing and panning gold. Rockerville, Dak. Old-timers, Spriggs,Lamb and Dillon at work. Photo and copyright by Crabill, 1889.

In early 1848, panning was the most popular method of mining for gold. Miners used pans to scoop up a bit of dirt from the riverbed, swirled water in the pan to rinse away the grit, and hoped a nugget or two would be left behind.

water would carry away the light sand and gravel, leaving heavier gold flakes behind in the pan's bottom. A miner could learn this technique in a matter of minutes.

WORKING TOGETHER

As long as panning was the favored mining method, most miners worked as individuals. An exception was miners who hired teams of Indians to work for them. At the beginning of the rush, in fact, a few men made fortunes using Indian laborers. Mason recorded that 50 Indians working for 6 miners on the Feather River had collected more than 270 pounds of gold for their employers.

By the fall of 1848, miners began to abandon the pan in favor of the cradle, a simple mechanism that they could make out of wood in about a day. About four to six feet in length, a cradle had a box at one end whose bottom was made from a perforated sheet of metal. On the other end was a long trough. Hammered into the trough was a series of narrow horizontal blocks called riffles.

To use a cradle, a miner shoveled dirt into the box and then poured water over it. The water pushed the dirt into the trough, and any big rocks were left behind on the box's metal bottom. As the dirt flowed over the trough, the light dirt particles were washed away and the heavier gold was caught on the riffles.

To operate a cradle, several men had to work together. Often, one shoveled the dirt, a second poured the water, a third rocked the cradle back and forth to keep the dirt flowing through it, and a fourth collected the gold from the riffles.

The cradle changed the nature of mining. Mining was no longer an individual enterprise; it was now a group effort, which required miners to form partnerships.

NEWCOMERS FROM OTHER LANDS

Another aspect of mining had also changed by the fall of 1848. Initially, the miners were mostly Americans and Californios who just happened to be nearby when news of the gold discovery first began to spread. Toward the end of the 1848 season, however, would-be miners from other locations started to make their way to California.

Thousands of American settlers from Oregon arrived after deciding to abandon their farms for the chance of a gold strike. Other miners came from farther away: There were soon Hawaiians, Chileans, and Mexicans from the state of Sonora working alongside the original Californians.

Surprisingly, there was little conflict among these groups. Everyone was too busy working his cradle to pay much attention

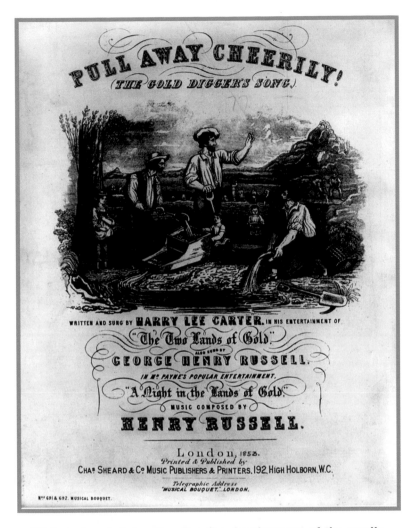

Mining changed greatly after the development of the cradle, which forced miners to work in teams instead of individually. The song "Pull Away Cheerily" is about miners using a cradle while searching for gold, as depicted by the cover of its sheet music *(above)*.

to anyone else—and at that point, no one was too worried about competition. With men finding fortunes every day, it seemed that there was plenty of gold for everyone.

A BUSINESS BOOM

As more and more men headed toward the mines, San Francisco was transformed. Most new miners arrived by ship and disembarked there. In less than a year, San Francisco went

"MUCH MORE THAN I ANTICIPATED"

Beginning in 1844, California entrepreneur Thomas Larkin served the U.S. government as the American consul in Monterey. In this capacity, Larkin first wrote to Secretary of State James Buchanan about the discovery of gold in California on June 1, 1848. A second letter to Buchanan, dated June 28, included more details. By this time, Larkin had visited the gold region himself and had seen with his own eyes what miners were digging from the riverbeds. This letter, which included Larkin's speculations about California's future, was widely reprinted and prompted many Americans to wonder whether those fantastic rumors of gold in the West could actually be true:

> Since the writing of [my earlier letter] I have visited a part of the gold region, and found it all I had heard, and much more than I anticipated. . . .
>
> I am of the opinion that on the American fork, Feather River, and Consumnes River, there are near two thousand people, nine-tenths of them foreigners. . . . I think there must, by this time, be over 1,000 men at work upon the different branches of the Sacramento; putting their gains at 10,000 dollars per day, for six days in the week, appears to me not overrated.
>
> Should this news reach the [men] of California and Oregon, . . . we should have a large addition to our population; and should the richness of the gold region continue, our

from being a backwater frontier town to a bustling city. With this lightning-fast growth, there were plenty of ways for men to make money. For instance, Sam Brannan, who had been instrumental in setting off the rush in the first place, found

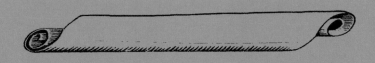

emigration in 1849 will be many thousands, and in 1850 still more. If our countrymen in California, as clerks, mechanics, and workmen, will forsake employment at from 2 dollars to 6 dollars per day, how many more of the same class in the Atlantic States, earning much less, will leave for this country under such prospects? It is the opinion of many who have visited the gold regions the past and present months, that the ground will afford gold for many years, perhaps for a century. . . .

How long this gathering of gold by the handful will continue here, or the future effect it will have on California, I cannot say. Three-fourths of the houses in the town on the bay of San Francisco are deserted. Houses are sold at the price of the ground lots. The effects are this week showing themselves in Monterey. Almost every house I had hired out is given up. Every blacksmith, carpenter, and lawyer is leaving; brick-yards, saw-mills and ranches are left perfectly alone. . . . A complete revolution in the ordinary state of affairs is taking place; both of our newspapers are discontinued from want of workmen and the loss of their agencies. . . .

If the affair proves a bubble, a mere excitement, I know not how we can all be deceived, as we are situated.[*]

---

[*]Thomas Larkin, *Letters to the Secretary of State About the Gold Discovery*. Available online. URL: http://www.sfmuseum.org/hist6/larkin.html.

himself swimming in riches by selling goods and services to experienced miners and new arrivals.

One business of Brannan's proved to be a failure. Before the rush, he had founded San Francisco's first newspaper, the *California Star*. In May 1848, Brannan was forced to shut it down because it had lost nearly all of its readers to the mines. Before closing the paper, however, Brannan published a special edition that breathlessly announced the discovery of gold in California: "The Great Sacramento Valley has a mine of gold. . . . From all accounts it is immensely rich and already we learn the gold from it, collected at random and without trouble, has become an article of trade. . . . This precious metal abounds in this country."[4] He printed 2,000 copies and loaded them on a wagon bound for Missouri. Brannan wanted the news to reach the eastern United States as soon as possible because he knew that promoting California and luring more miners there could only be good for business.

SPREADING THE NEWS

Brannan's plan worked. When his special edition was distributed, the news spread fast and was reprinted in local papers and city dailies alike. By August, newspapers throughout the East were reporting on California gold.

Not all of the reports were glowing. In many locales, the newspapers were a dog-eat-dog business. Some papers claimed that gold rumors were all lies just to discredit rival newspapers that were reporting them as fact. A few insisted that the gold was a fib invented by President Polk to justify his expensive war with Mexico.

Generally, Americans were at first skeptical. They had a hard time believing the reports of the California gold find because, frankly, they seemed unbelievable. The United States was still largely a nation of farmers, and Americans were used to the idea of making a living by working the land.

In farming, however, to make even a modest return required a great deal of hard work. The idea of collecting a quick fortune by picking up gold from riverbeds seemed too good to be true.

Still, stories of gold in California kept coming. Reports from Thomas Larkin sent to Secretary of State James Buchanan were published in the *New York Herald* and picked up by smaller papers. People in the states also began to receive letters from friends and relatives in California that confirmed the wildest of the rumors.

PRESIDENT POLK SPEAKS

Public opinion did not completely turn until after mid-September, when a letter from Governor Mason arrived in Washington, D.C. Mailed in July, it included a lengthy report of Mason's own tour of the mines, an awe-inspiring description of the ongoing gold strikes. Given the accusations that the rumors were all part of a conspiracy cooked up by Polk, Mason knowingly included a passage designed to please the president. He wrote that California contained so much gold that it "would pay the cost of the present war with Mexico a hundred times over."[5]

Mason certainly seemed to be a reliable source of information, but his words were not what impressed Americans most. What did was the contents of a package he sent with his letter: a sample of California gold worth almost $4,000. The government placed it on public display at the War Department.

At last, Polk was ready to speak out publicly about the matter. On December 5, 1848, he delivered a state of the union message to Congress. In it, the president, in no uncertain terms, declared that California was full of gold: "Recent discoveries render it probable that these mines are more extensive and valuable than was anticipated. The accounts of the abundance of gold in that territory are of such an extraordinary character as would scarcely command belief were they not corroborated by the authentic reports of officers in the public service."[6]

In an instant, the president's words changed the debate over California. People were no longer asking, "Are the gold rumors true?" They were now asking, "Should I stay or should I go?"

Getting There

In January 1849, the *New York Herald* announced that all of New York City had been overtaken by a new and devastating disorder—gold mania. As the paper explained, "All classes of our citizens seem to be under the influence of this extraordinary mania [that] exceeds everything in the history of commercial adventure."[1]

Other newspapers across the country used similar language to describe Americans' fascination with California gold. Most commonly, they called it "gold fever," acknowledging that the eagerness to head out for the mines seemed contagious. Once one man in a community caught the fever, it tended to spread quickly, until just about every family knew someone who had come down with it.

HOPING FOR A FORTUNE

Although the mass media tried to depict "gold fever" as some strange affliction, most men approached their decision about going to California carefully and rationally. The great majority of Americans who chose to head west did it for one reason— money. For poor young men with few prospects, the decision was fairly easy. With little to lose, taking a risk on California seemed like a smart move.

At the time, a farm hand might make one dollar per day, and a skilled craftsman might be able to pocket $1.50. In California, miners were averaging $16 a day in gold; the luckiest miners could take in far more. Not surprisingly, newspapers, eager to draw in readers, loved to share sensational stories of fantastic strikes that yielded fortunes of tens or even hundreds of thousands of dollars.

Even with the powerful lure of easy wealth, older, more established men generally had a hard time deciding whether to head west. They had farms or businesses to take care of and likely had wives, children, and elderly relatives who depended on them and their income. Yet the possibility of making a great deal of money very quickly was overpoweringly attractive to many middle-class men. If they stayed, they could expect to work long hours for the rest of their lives, often at jobs that were physically exhausting. If they left, they at least had a chance of acquiring enough wealth that they could give up back-breaking labor once and for all and still be able to provide a good life for their family.

CONVINCING THE FAMILY

Every would-be miner hoped to find a pile of gold. Some, however, also had additional reasons to head to California. Many men, especially young ones, saw it as a great adventure, a chance for fun and excitement. Others viewed it as a means of escape. They longed to get away from boring jobs, overbearing parents, or family responsibilities.

Those who saw going to California as a way to flee their present lives rarely shared these feelings with others, especially their relatives. Instead, they justified their decisions by saying that they were only thinking of what would be best for the family. One miner named Harvey Chapman used this strategy to persuade his wife to approve of his trip to the mines: "[Y]ou think of me very wild for going away from my Sweet baby & affectionate wife & mild & Pleasant mother in law & Clever daddy in law but nothing but gold would take me away."[2]

This argument did not always calm disapproving family members. Many wives were understandably angry that their husbands even considered going to California. They did not want to be left alone to care for their children, often with limited financial means. Parents also often resisted their sons' eagerness to the leave. At the time, older people looked to their children for financial and emotional support. Many parents, therefore, felt that their sons were trying to worm out of their obligations to care for them. Mothers were especially hostile to the idea of their sons leaving home, as the letter of one miner attests: "Mother o Mother, why do you still resist my going my mind is made up to go. Why o why cant you let me go with a cherful heart, and with a well made up mind that i will try to do well."[3]

Men were also subject to criticism from community leaders. Clergymen especially railed against the lure of California. Many preached that risking life and limb in search of gold was wrong. They also cautioned that California society was so decadent that it could lead an otherwise moral man astray. Some prominent intellectuals, however, argued that Americans had a moral obligation to go to California to spread their values in this new part of the country. This idea of the need to "Americanize" California particularly appealed to Protestants with a prejudice against Catholicism, the religion of California's Mexican population.

MONEY AND EMOTION

After deep consideration, tens of thousands of Americans decided to try their luck in California in the early months of 1849. These "49ers" then turned to the practical matter of

"THEM STORIES ABOUT... CALIFORNY WAS ALL TRUE"

Prentice Mulford (1834–1891) was a noted author and journalist who was also known for his comic lecturers. In 1889, he wrote *Prentice Mulford's Story: Life by Land and Sea,* a memoir of his travels to California and his life there between 1856 and 1872. In this excerpt from his book, Mulford remembers how news of the California gold find spread gold fever throughout his hometown of Sag Harbor, New York, in the summer of 1848.

> One June morning, when I was a boy, Captain Eben Latham came to our house, and the first gossip he unloaded was, that "them stories about finding gold in Californy was all true." . . . That was the first report I heard from California. Old Eben had been a man of the sea; was once captured by a pirate, and when he told the story, which he did once a week, he concluded by rolling up his trousers and showing the bullet-scars he had received.
>
> California then was but a blotch of yellow on the schoolboy's map of 1847. . . . By November, 1848, California was the talk of the village, as it was all that time of the whole country. The great gold fever raged all winter.
>
> All the old retired whaling captains wanted to go, and most of them did go. All the spruce young men of the place wanted to go. Companies were formed, and there was much serious drawing up of constitutions and by-laws for their regulation. . . . The

planning the trip. The first and biggest hurdle for most was financial. They not only had to fund their own travel west. They also had to ensure that their dependent relatives had a way to make ends meet while they were away.

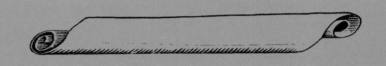

companies bought safes, in which to keep their gold, and also strange and complex gold-washing machines, of which numerous patterns suddenly sprang up, invented by Yankees who never saw and never were to see a gold mine. . . . People with the lightning glance and divination of golden anticipation, saw themselves already in the mines hauling over chunks of ore and returning home weighed down with them. . . .

As the winter of "'48" waned the companies, one after another, set sail for the land of gold. The Sunday preceding they listened to farewell sermons at church. . . . They were admonished from the pulpit to behave temperately, virtuously, wisely, and piously. . . . How patiently and resignedly they listened to the sad discourse of the minister, knowing it would be the last they would hear for many months. How eager the glances they cast up to the church choir, where sat the girls they were to marry on their return. How few returned. How few married the girl of that period's choice. How little weighed the words of the minister a year afterward in the hurry-scurry of the San Francisco life of '49 and '50.[*]

[*]Prentice Mulford, *Prentice Mulford's Story: Life by Land and Sea.* New York: F.J. Needham, 1889. Available online. URL: memory.loc.gov/cgi-bin/query/r?ammem/calbk:@field(DOCID+@lit(calbk050div2)).

Most miners did not have enough savings to pay all these expenses. Many had to borrow from family and friends. Others sold or mortgaged their houses to make enough. A miner's family often moved into cheaper living quarters. Sometimes, a wife had to learn about the family business, be it a farm or a shop, so she could keep it running while her husband was gone.

Miners also had to prepare themselves and their families emotionally for their absence. They often counseled their children to behave well and study hard while they were away. Many were also concerned that their children would forget about them. One miner who hoped to keep himself in his young son's thoughts wanted the boy to learn to say "Papa is coming home bye & bye."[4] Some miners also feared that their wives would be unfaithful. One man instructed his wife on proper behavior, telling her "on no account receive male visitors in your rooms."[5] He claimed he was just worried about what "strangers" might think, but he was clearly more than a little anxious about what she might do when he was not around.

IN IT TOGETHER

Most men who left for California in early 1849 did not go alone. Instead, they joined companies of miners who pooled their money and traveled west together. Most companies had about 30 to 50 men, although large ones could have 200 members.

Many guidebooks and countless articles about California were available, but even so, the miners sensed that they did not, and could not, know what their lives in California were going to be like. By forming mining companies with friends and relatives, they felt more secure about heading into the unknown.

Relatives of the miners also felt better knowing that the miners would be traveling to California with other men from

Above, a cartoonist humorously depicts the mad dash to California during the gold rush.

their communities. Not only would the miners be surrounded by familiar faces, but they could also keep an eye on each other and report back to loved ones any bad behavior.

The miners themselves were also concerned about the temptations they would face. To protect themselves and each other, they wrote elaborate constitutions for their companies. These often forbade members to swear, drink alcohol, and gamble.

THE ROUTES TO CALIFORNIA

Companies also had to select the route that they would take to California. In 1849, there were three main options—a long sea route around Cape Horn at the southern tip of South America, a shorter sea route that included an overland trek across the isthmus of Panama, and a land route along the Oregon and California trails.

A company's starting point largely determined whether it set out by sea or land. Ships bound for San Francisco sailed out of eastern port cities such as New York and Boston. The trails west began at towns along the Missouri River such as St. Joseph and Independence in Missouri. Generally, if a company came from an area relatively close to the Atlantic Ocean, it took a sea route. If a company came from a community located much farther inland, it took the land route.

There were other considerations as well. Taking a ship was more expensive, but it was more comfortable. A passenger could also carry more cargo.

Timing was another factor. Ships could set sail as soon as the winter storms ended in January or February. The journey around the Cape took about five months, though, whereas the Panama route took about six weeks. Either way, a miner traveling by sea could get to California in time to take advantage of the 1849 mining season.

Miners who traveled overland, however, had to wait until May before leaving. Only then would grass on the Great Plains be high enough to feed the overlanders' oxen along the way. They would not reach California until about November. By that time, the winter rains were about to set in, thus making mining impossible until the next year.

No matter which route a company took, the entire community came out to give the men a great send-off the day they began their trip. Bands played as the crowd waved flags and handkerchiefs. Prominent citizens gave speeches, urging the miners to work hard and make everyone back home proud.

AROUND THE CAPE

In 1849, most miners who took a sea route chose to travel around Cape Horn. The trip was the longer of the two sea routes, but many men were afraid to travel across Panama. They had all heard stories of outbreaks of yellow fever and other deadly diseases there. Miners were risk takers, but even so, many did not want to chance dying from disease before they even got to California.

The worst thing about the cape route was the length of the voyage. Except for the occasional stop at a port, each day was much like the last. The travelers put on plays, held dances, and marched in military drills—anything they could think of to relieve the tedium. Boredom drove some companies' members to drink and gamble despite their pledges to refrain from these vices.

Not surprisingly, living in close quarters also began to wear on morale. Petty gripes and arguments quickly eroded the sense of brotherhood they had felt at the beginning of their journey. As Enoch Jacobs wrote in his journal, "God Grant us a breeze soon for these long Calms are fruitful in producing dissension and disaffections."[6]

ACROSS PANAMA

Taking the Panama route shaved months off the travel time. Crossing the isthmus was also an exciting experience. Miners were amazed to see monkeys, alligators, and parrots and were delighted by the beautiful sunrises and sunsets in the tropics.

Although most of the trip over the isthmus could be taken by boat, there was a 26-mile stretch that had to be traveled on foot. After a grueling trek over winding muddy trails, the miners finally arrived in Panama City. From there, they were to catch steamers to take them north to San Francisco.

In 1849, there were too few steamboats and too many miners. Some miners found themselves stuck camping on the beach in Panama City for weeks. While they waited, they not only worried about catching a disease, but also about the time they were wasting. One man wrote in his diary about meeting "a returning Californian . . . with a box containing $22,000 in gold dust and a four pound lump in one hand." He noted that his "impatience and excitement . . . already at a high pitch were greatly increased."[7]

ON THE TRAIL

The miners who traveled overland had a much different experience. While aboard ship, those on the sea routes just had to find some way to amuse themselves to make the time pass more quickly. The overlanders, however, had to work hard, day in and day out. Every day but the Sabbath, they traveled as far as they could along the trail on foot or aboard a covered wagon.

Even after overlanders set up camp for the night, they faced hours of exhausting labor. A miner named Henry Packer described the routine: "In the evening, after stopping, the horses are to offgear, tie up, currey, and feed and water; the tent is put up—bed clothes to arrange, supper to prepare and eat—which last is not hard to do—by this time it is bed time, and we 'turn in.' Then again, each member of the company comes upon guard duty once every fourth or fifth night."[8]

The overlanders were proud of their ability to deal with the difficulties of trail life, and they looked down on miners who traveled by sea, mocking them as soft and weak. The overland trip also allowed them marvel at beautiful western landscapes and to just spend time in the open air. One man from Pennsylvania wrote that being on the trail "is far more pleasing to me than to sit daily locked up in a dirty office. Besides the pleasure of the thing, it gives us health and strength. I can sleep in the tent or wagon far better than I could in a bed, no roaches to disturb us at midnight and no bell to call us to breakfast."[9]

However they traveled, all of the miners who set out for California in 1849 shared one thing—a sense that they were part of a great national experience. Many wrote about their travels in diaries and letters. Writing down their stories not only helped them kill time at sea or enjoy a quiet moment of reflection after a long day on the trail, it also allowed them to record their part in what they already saw as a great American adventure. One miner, a doctor from Michigan, warned his family that in his letters he would not be able to give an account of everything that happened to him. He added that, when he had the opportunity to write everything down "I will give you enough to satisfy you that 1849 will ever be a memorable epoch in the history of our country. Neither the Crusades nor Alexander's expeditions to India can equal this emigration to California."[10]

In the Mines

"Every heart beats high as we near the Golden Shore. All is speculation, expectation & anticipation."[1] A 49er named Charles Buckingham used these words to describe his excitement as his ship sailed into San Francisco Bay. For all miners, spying the "Golden Shore" was an exhilarating moment. They had spent weeks planning the move to California and then months traveling under difficult conditions to get there. Now they were finally in California, ready at last to grab their share of the riches it promised.

Along with excitement, many miners felt trepidation. Their long journey to California had come to an end, but their adventure in this strange place was just beginning. One miner explained the anxiety he felt when it came time to leave his ship and step into a new world: "Notwithstanding all our discomforts, it cost me a pang to leave the steamer. It seemed like

Mining towns like Placerville *(above)* popped up in California as more and more people flooded the state in search of gold. People who traveled by land usually ended up in Placerville, which became an important supply center for the region's mining camps.

cutting loose the last tie that bound me to home & friends, & found myself indeed alone & entirely dependent upon myself for everything."[2]

THE HIGH COST OF CALIFORNIA

Before going to the mines, new arrivals had to buy the food and supplies they would need. Overlanders gathered at the mining town of Placerville. Miners who traveled by sea came together in the bustling city of San Francisco.

No matter where they were, miners were stunned by their first introduction to California prices. In the early years of the rush, when just about every able-bodied man was consumed by mining, most goods available in California had to be imported from the eastern United States or from another country. The cost of transportation and the scarcity of goods drove prices sky high.

Housing and restaurant meals were especially expensive. The opulent Parker House in the center of San Francisco rented small rooms at $1800 a month (roughly $36,000 in today's money). A miner named E. Gould Buffum recorded that he and a friend spent $43 on breakfast at a boardinghouse one morning. The same meal would have cost about 25 cents before the rush began.

OUTFITTING THE MINER

Although they flinched at the high prices, miners had to buy supplies regardless of the cost. They had to have certain basic mining tools, such as a shovel, a pick, and a pan or a cradle. They also needed items necessary for survival in mining camps, including a tent, a blanket, a kettle, a baking pan, a lamp, and a hatchet.

Miners also brought foodstuffs with them, because there was no guarantee that they would be able to buy these at the rough towns that had sprung up around mining camps. The miners' diet was fairly bland: It was generally limited to preserved beef and pork, beans, and bread. Tea and coffee, sweetened with sugar, were also a part of nearly every meal.

Miners also had to buy work clothing. Because they would spend much of their mining time wading in rivers, boots were the most important part of the miner's attire. Sturdy boots were in such high demand that even a used pair might sell for $50. Just about every miner also wore a checkered shirt and canvas pants.

The last element of the miner's uniform was the cheapest—a long beard. Men who would be embarrassed to be seen with a hint of stubble back home were proud of their scruffy facial hair. They may have once been farmers, shopkeepers, or undertakers, but, once their beards grew in, they felt that they had transformed into something else. They were now officially miners.

All miners grumbled at the price of these goods, but most were completely stunned by the cost of transporting them. In 1849, a miner in San Francisco might pay $100 for supplies and then another $100 to get them out to the mines.

HEADING FOR THE GOLD FIELDS

The mining region was divided into two areas—the northern mines and the southern mines. From San Francisco, two rivers provided access to these areas. Miners bound for the northern mines took steamships up the Sacramento River to the town of Sacramento. Those bound for the southern mines headed up the San Joaquin River to the town of Stockton.

From Sacramento and Stockton, miners set out overland to the mines. Some traveled on foot with their cargo carried by pack mules; others took stagecoaches over dirt trails. Overstuffed with people and supplies, the coaches were smelly inside, and most passengers preferred riding on the coach's roofs so they could breathe the fresh air.

During the trip to the northern gold country, many miners were overwhelmed by the beautiful mountain vistas and pine forests. One miner from Maine was especially struck by the vegetation that covered valleys and hills as the mining season began. He wrote, "O how butiful it seems in the morning to git up and hear the birds of Spring and to look around on the distant hill and see them covered with flowers it is a site worth seeing there is not a spear of grass without there is a flower on it."[3]

CAMP LIFE

When the miners reached the gold region, they settled into one of the dozens of mining camps located along rivers and tributaries. Each camp had a name. Some were named after the first miner to make a big strike there. Others—such as Rough and Ready, Loafer Hill, and Murderer's Bar—hinted at the harsh and even dangerous aspects of camp life.

Sometimes, miners built a log cabin to live in, but most settled for a tent or a simple shelter thrown together from tree branches. They did not want to take time away from mining to construct something more permanent. Besides, miners generally did not think that they were in California for the long haul. Each dreamed of making a quick and easy fortune and leaving the rough world of California as a rich man.

After 1848, miners rarely worked alone. Once the cradle had become the dominant mining tool, men were compelled to work in teams. Teamwork was even more necessary after the introduction of the long tom.

This device was similar to the cradle, but longer, measuring as much as 15 feet in length. With an increased number of riffles, the long tom caught more gold than the cradle. By 1850, miners had improved the long tom by rubbing the riffles with mercury, a metal that attracted gold.

Usually, a miner met his partners soon after arriving in the West. More often than not, the companies that miners joined back home fell apart once they reached California. The tensions brought out during the long journey or just the desire to start fresh led many men to abandon old friends and seek out new ones.

FINDING A CLAIM

Before a team could start mining, it first had to establish a claim—that is, an area along a river where it had an exclusive right to mine. In 1848, miners could stake a claim

Few men who flocked to California during the Gold Rush expected to stay there long. Some miners built log cabins, but most slept in tents or rough shelters made from tree branches.

just by leaving a pick stuck in the ground. Others searching for a claim would see the pick and know that they had to look elsewhere.

After that first season, however, the number of miners in California exploded. By the end of 1848, there were about 5,000. By the end of 1849, there were almost 40,000, and year after year, more kept coming. The more miners there were, the more competition there was for good claims. Claims also became smaller. In 1848, claims were often as big as 1,000 square feet. Just two years later, they had shrunk to as little as 15 square feet.

With the growing competition for claims, a team of miners often had to buy a claim, usually on credit. Even before they had washed their first pail of dirt, they found themselves deep in debt. Decreasing access to claims also led to an increase in stealing claims, which the miners called "claim jumping." Disputes between miners over who owned a claim were common and were usually decided by informal tribunals of miners that organized in the camps to settle disagreements.

Miners did not look kindly on claim jumpers, but gold thieves were even more despised. With no police force in the mining region, miners took it on themselves to deal with men accused of stealing: They quickly cobbled together juries to weigh the evidence, and if the accused was found guilty, punishment was equally swift. Usually, thieves were whipped and banished from the mining camp. Murderers were often hanged.

THE MINER'S DAY

In California, dispensing justice was speedy for one reason—men did not welcome any distraction from mining. Every day but Sunday, they labored for long hours under grueling conditions. Newcomers were often stunned by the physical demands of the job. As one miner explained, "[T]he incredible difficulties and hardships attending the operations of mining are no more understood in the United States than the hieroglyphics of the pyramids.... The digging and washing processes are the hardest kind of work a human being ever performed."[4]

Once they got over their initial shock, most miners accepted the realities of gold mining and its wear and tear on the body. Bayard Taylor, a journalist who reported on the Gold Rush, recounted how he overcame his distaste for the intense physical labor involved: "When I first saw the men carrying heavy stones in the sun, standing nearly waist-deep in water, grubbing with their hands in the gravel and clay, there seemed to me little virtue in gold-digging. But when the shining particles were poured out lavishly from a tin basin, I confess there was a sudden itching in my fingers to seize the heaviest crowbar and the biggest shovel."[5]

A miner's day started early. Before the sun rose, miners got out of bed, ate breakfast, and drank coffee. With the day's first light, they gathered up their shovels, buckets, and other supplies and headed out for their claim. They worked for about five hours before breaking for lunch. The partners then returned to their claim and continued to work until about an hour before sunset. They calculated their gold take for the day, packed up their supplies, and trudged back to their cabin or tent.

After an exhausting day, every miner welcomed suppertime. Usually, the men took turns cooking. As the cook for the day busily prepared dinner, the rest of the team built a fire, took off their wet boots, and relaxed. The foods served differed little from day to day. They generally included some kind of meat, either dried or freshly hunted, and almost always bread. In their journals, miners often recorded with glee their first successful attempt to bake a loaf.

After dinner, the men would laze around the fire. As they smoked pipes or cigars, one might read out loud from a book, a newspaper, or a letter from home. Other times, the men would just talk, telling each other about their lives back home and about what they would do once they made their big gold strike.

RELAXING ON THE SABBATH

In California, many miners quickly forgot their promises to their families not to drink, smoke, and swear, but nearly all continued to observe the Sabbath. A few spent the day reading the Bible or listening to sermons by traveling preachers. Most miners, however, just took advantage of this religious convention to take a day off work.

Many devoted their Sundays to chores. They took baths, washed their clothes, or wrote entries in their diaries or letters home. In the highly social world of the mining camps, some sneaked in a little time to be by themselves. They might wander through the countryside or just stay in their tents to read and relax.

THE MINER'S TEN COMMANDMENTS

During the Gold Rush, many miners wrote to their loved ones on pictorial letter sheets. These writing papers were similar to picture postcards: They featured a picture, as well as a space for a message, and could be folded and mailed at the lowest postage rate. Hundreds of scenes were available on pictorial sheets, with images that ranged from downtown San Francisco to lovely California landscapes to miners at work. The most popular included a list of rules for life in California called "The Miner's Ten Commandments," which is excerpted below. This pictorial letter sheet sold nearly 100,000 copies.

I. Thou shalt have no other claim than one.

II. Thou shalt not make unto thyself any false claim, nor any likeness to a mean man, by jumping one. . . .

III. Thou shalt not go prospecting before thy claim gives out. Neither shalt thou take thy money, nor thy gold dust, nor thy good name, to the gaming table in vain. . . .

IV. Thou shalt not remember what thy friends do at home on the Sabbath day, lest the remembrance may not compare favorably with what thou doest here. . . .

V. Though shalt not think more of all thy gold, and how thou canst make it fastest, than how thou will enjoy it after thou hast ridden rough-shod over thy good old parents' precepts and examples. . . .

Others sought out less wholesome entertainment and visited the makeshift towns that sprouted up in the mining region. There, miners could get a drink at a saloon or a meal at a

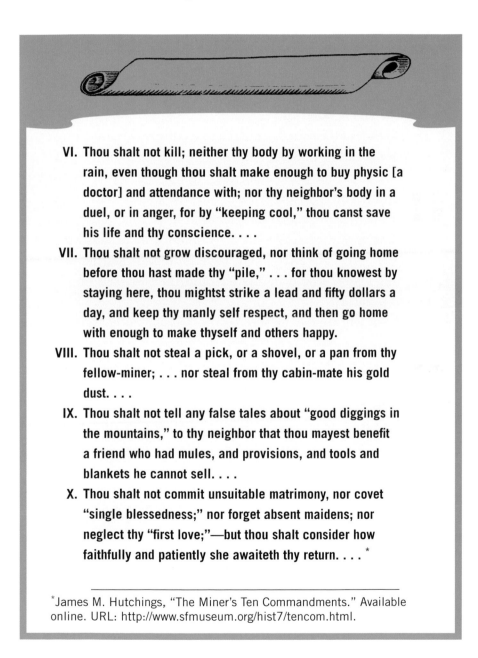

VI. Thou shalt not kill; neither thy body by working in the rain, even though thou shalt make enough to buy physic [a doctor] and attendance with; nor thy neighbor's body in a duel, or in anger, for by "keeping cool," thou canst save his life and thy conscience. . . .

VII. Thou shalt not grow discouraged, nor think of going home before thou hast made thy "pile," . . . for thou knowest by staying here, thou mightst strike a lead and fifty dollars a day, and keep thy manly self respect, and then go home with enough to make thyself and others happy.

VIII. Thou shalt not steal a pick, or a shovel, or a pan from thy fellow-miner; . . . nor steal from thy cabin-mate his gold dust. . . .

IX. Thou shalt not tell any false tales about "good diggings in the mountains," to thy neighbor that thou mayest benefit a friend who had mules, and provisions, and tools and blankets he cannot sell. . . .

X. Thou shalt not commit unsuitable matrimony, nor covet "single blessedness;" nor forget absent maidens; nor neglect thy "first love;"—but thou shalt consider how faithfully and patiently she awaiteth thy return. . . . *

*James M. Hutchings, "The Miner's Ten Commandments." Available online. URL: http://www.sfmuseum.org/hist7/tencom.html.

boardinghouse. They might play a game of billiards or ten-pin bowling. Sometimes, towns featured traveling shows and circuses or, in southern mines, bullfights. To the more religiously minded miners, the most disturbing thing about the towns were their crude gambling halls. These men were stunned to watch their friends and partners gamble away earnings on a day that they felt should be devoted to the Lord.

COPING WITH WINTER

The rhythm of life continued unchanged throughout the mining season, but by mid-September, in anticipation of the winter rains, all the men in the northern mines had to prepare for the season's end. For some, the end of the season marked the end of their California adventure. Even if they had not made their fortunes, they might be too homesick or exhausted to continue. Others or they might have promised their families that this season would be the last and therefore felt honor-bound to return.

Those who opted to stay had a decision to make. One choice was to head for the southern mines to try their luck. There, the rainy season came in the spring. They could spend the winter digging up dirt, which they would then wash once the spring rains began. Another choice was to go to San Francisco or Sacramento to look for wage work as laborers, clerks, or waiters. The wages would not make these miners rich, but at least they could be earning something during the off-season.

A third option was staying put in the mining region. This decision required careful planning. Before the rains came, miners had to find adequate shelter to weather the coldest months. They had to either build new cabins or improve those they already had. They also had to buy enough supplies to last through the winter. The rains turned the dirt roads that led to Sacramento into mud pits that were far too dangerous to travel.

WORRIES AND DOUBTS

Even a warm cabin and a hoard of supplies were not enough to keep a miner comfortable during the rainy season. Few could prepare themselves for the psychological toll of waiting out the winter. After months of hard labor and intense social interactions, they found themselves largely cut off from human contact with nothing to do day after day.

Left with too much time alone with their thoughts, many men began to dwell on their troubles and to drown in self-doubt. Through the mining season, a man could choke down worries about failure by reminding himself that if he did not make his fortune today, there was always tomorrow. Through the long winter, however, stuck in an isolated camp with a few other stragglers, a miner had a harder time bucking himself up. Try as he might, he would think back on the high hopes that had brought him west and on the desperation for success that had kept him there. Such troubling thoughts no doubt led some miners to wish that they had never heard of California gold.

A New Way
of Living

"Every newcomer in San Francisco is overtaken with a sense of complete bewilderment,"[1] wrote Gold Rush journalist Bayard Taylor. Certainly, in the first few seasons of the rush, the city went though a transformation that impressed and unsettled both small-town boys and big-city sophisticates.

Many commented on the dizzying mix of structures found along San Francisco's streets. A four-story brick building might stand next to a store that consisted of nothing but a tent with a few wooden planks set up as display racks. These odd juxtapositions testified to the city's unplanned, free-form existence. Even from day to day, everything seemed to change in unordered and unpredictable ways. For many Americans, used to rural life that altered little from generation to generation, this whirlwind of change was disorienting.

Even more daunting was the miners' sense that they were in a new type of society, one that previously had existed nowhere in America or even on Earth. Both in San Francisco and in the mines, they found a social world in which old rules of conduct and morality no longer applied. When men left their homes for California, they knew that they would face physical challenges during their journey and while working in the mines, but most were unprepared for the difficult psychological struggle of negotiating California's confusing social world.

LOOKING OUT FOR NUMBER ONE

Part of this challenge involved gold itself. Most American Christians at the time had been taught from childhood to be suspicious of greed. As miners left their homes in search of gold, they therefore had to rationalize what they were doing. They told themselves that they were not abandoning their loved ones because they were greedy; instead, they recast it as a selfless act, a great sacrifice that they were making for the good of their families.

Once in California, however, it was more difficult to hide the thirst for wealth that had driven them west. Gold was everywhere, getting rich was the favorite topic of conversation, and the inflated prices were evidence of everyone's willingness to take advantage of others. The climate led many men to rethink selfishness. What was once a vice now seemed a simple mode of self-preservation. As a miner named Thomas Forbes wrote, "It is every man for himself and the devil for them all. I am looking out for number one."[2]

Unsurprisingly, gold-rich California allowed men to explore many other vices as well. Without parents or wives looking over their shoulders, for the first time, men had the opportunity to indulge in behavior that would be condemned back home. Everywhere in California, liquor flowed freely.

Away from family and strict values, gold seekers quickly adjusted to the wild, boozy atmosphere of San Francisco *(above)*. Gambling and adultery were rampant here, and card playing, brawling, and laughter filled the saloons of the city.

Many miners who had been committed teetotalers became saloon regulars. Gambling houses likewise attracted successful miners, giving them a chance to win another fortune or to lose it all. Prostitutes were available in larger numbers than anywhere else.

FINDING FRIENDS

A few men seized the chance to recreate themselves in this new and strange environment. Bored with their former lives or frustrated by their family obligations, they resolved never to go back home. Many severed their ties to old friends and began to call themselves by new names. California proved to be an easy place to erase the past, to create a new life for oneself, to begin again with the slate wiped clean.

For most men, however, living in a world of strangers was hardly exhilarating. As mining companies broke up and men lost contact with people they knew from home, they grew anxious, fearful of dealing with a rough and often frightening world alone. For security, they actively sought out new friends.

Often in the mines, partners developed extremely close friendships. By its very nature, mining was a highly competitive business. Just having partners rooting for their shared success was itself a comfort. Even more important, these mining friendships assured men that they would have someone they could count on if they became ill or just needed another person to confide in. Also testifying to the intensity of these relationships was the bitter reaction miners sometimes had when friends decided to leave California without them. One diarist wrote angrily of the end of a tight friendship: "So I bade him good bye &c, & he went on promises of sticking together of taking care of one another &c. . . . All vanished into 'thin air' at the moment of trial."[3]

When a miner went home, he often stayed in touch with his former partners. Families often had trouble understanding the closeness of these bonds that their loved ones had with men that they might have known only for a few months.

A MULTICULTURAL SOCIETY

American miners bonded not only over their need for mutual support, but also over their mutual dislike of foreigners.

As early as 1848, a few foreign miners, mostly from Mexico and Hawaii, trickled into the gold fields. In 1849, as word spread to Europe and beyond, foreigners began to flood into California.

The majority of European miners came from Ireland, which was experiencing a devastating famine, and from France, which was embroiled in political upheaval. A large number of miners also came from Central and South America, including Mexicans, Chileans, and Peruvians. Australians began to arrive late in the 1849 season.

The 1852 season saw a massive migration of miners from China. In that year alone, at least 25,000 Chinese men came to San Francisco. The Chinese tended to keep to themselves, often patiently working claims that other miners had given up.

This influx of men from around the world made California one of the most diverse societies in the world. A miner from Boston was dumbstruck by seeing men of so many different nationalities and cultures. He wrote that San Francisco seemed like a type of city "the world never produced before. Crowded with . . . Yankees & the Chinaman jostling each other in the streets, while French, Germans, Sandwich Islanders, Chilians, Malays, Mexicans, &c &c in all their varieties of costume and language go to form a congrommoration of humanity."[4]

PREJUDICES, OLD AND NEW

Few Americans shared this miner's enthusiasm for the multiculturalism of California. Much of their hostility was born out of old prejudices. From birth, Americans of the time were taught to look down on people from other countries, even if their parents or relatives were recent immigrants.

In California, though, these long-held prejudices were stoked by Americans' anger over having to compete with foreigners for gold claims. In 1848, Americans generally left foreign miners alone. Only in later seasons, when there were more miners and less gold, did Americans began to rail against outsiders.

Most commonly, they argued that, because California was now part of the United States, the gold there belonged only to Americans. This idea was bolstered by the fact that gold was discovered only days before California was formally transferred to the United States. Many Americans believed that God was behind this coincidence: They claimed that God wanted the gold to belong to Americans; therefore, if they allowed foreigners to snatch it, they would be acting against God's will.

STRIKING OUT

American hostility toward foreigners often erupted into violence. For instance, after a Fourth of July celebration in 1849, bands of Americans attacked Chileans in the streets of San Francisco. Americans especially resented Chileans because many were experienced miners. Their sheer competence in the mines fueled hatred toward them.

Californians also used taxes to drive foreigners out of the mines. In April 1850, they levied a $20 per month tax on all non-American miners for the "privilege of taking from our country the vast treasure to which they have no right."[5] The tax was high enough to make some foreign miners give up and go home. Sometimes, Americans claimed, rightly or wrongly, that a particular miner had not paid the tax. They then used that as a pretext to seize the miner's gold and possessions, essentially putting him out of business.

The tax on foreign miners had an unexpected consequence, however. As it drove foreigners away, it endangered the livelihoods of American merchants who sold them goods. Merchants in the southern mines particularly depended on Mexican customers for their profits. Because of these merchants' complaints, the tax was repealed in March 1851.

HOSTILITY TOWARD INDIANS

Americans reserved their most extreme contempt for one group of "foreigners"—the Indian peoples who had lived in California hundreds of years before Americans had ever set foot there. Unlike foreign miners, Indians did not present any competition. Some worked in the mines in 1848, usually as hired employees of Americans, but after the first season, Indians were largely absent from the mines.

Fearing non-Indians, most Indian peoples retreated into remote areas to avoid them. As the gold fields grew in size,

JOAQUIN MURIETA
(C. 1829–1853)

Gold Rush Outlaw

Captain Harry Love led a crew of men that hunted down and killed Mexican thieves, including one whose severed head they preserved in a jar of whiskey. The head was displayed in California for the next 50 years. It was said to belong to the legendary bandit Joaquin Murieta.

From 1851 to 1853, this notorious bandit terrorized the southern mining region of California. He stole cattle, held up stagecoaches, and murdered without conscience. The state legislature finally took action by offering a $1,000 bounty on Joaquin, who could be taken dead or alive.

Little is known about the real Joaquin Murieta. In fact, some historians claim that he did not even exist. Even so, Murieta played an important role in Gold Rush history. He became a symbol of the mistreatment suffered by Mexicans and other minorities at the hands of white Americans during this period.

however, they had fewer places to hide. In addition, the miners were taking over their habitat, making it difficult for Indians to gain access to plant and animal resources that had traditionally sustained them.

Suffering from disease and starvation, Indians sometimes raided farms established by Americans and stole crops and livestock. Americans retaliated with horrific violence against any Indians they could find, not caring whether or not they were the guilty parties. Disappointed miners also often took their anxiety out on Indians, whom Americans barely regarded

The legend of Joaquin Murieta largely comes from *The Life and Adventures of Joaquin Murieta, the Celebrated California Bandit* (1854), a book by Cherokee writer John Rollin Ridge. The horrors that the Cherokee Indians had suffered in Georgia under U.S. soldiers and civilians in the 1830s echoed throughout his account of Murieta's life. According to Ridge, Murieta traveled from Mexico to work in the southern mines but was beaten and driven away by American miners. When an American raped his wife, Murieta turned into a vigilante. Heading a band of outlaws, he sought revenge for the degradations that he and, by extension, all Mexicans, faced in California.

This story of Murieta, often called California's Robin Hood, had romantic appeal, but it also touched a nerve with both American and foreign miners, many of whom were appalled by the violence and prejudice that ran rampant through the mining region. Murieta's story has since been told dozens of times in ballads, plays, poems, and films. To this day, he remains a popular folk hero among Hispanic Americans in the American West.

as human. Knowing that there would be no retribution, otherwise decent men committed atrocities against weakened Indian groups. They routinely murdered Indians for no reason and kidnapped and raped Indian women and girls.

A WORLD WITHOUT WOMEN

The social world of the Gold Rush was not only distinguished by the presence of non-Americans. It was also unique for what it lacked—namely, women. Some wives accompanied their husbands to the gold fields, but they were few and far between. In California, men were more likely to encounter Mexican women, Indian women, and women who worked as saloon girls or prostitutes. Even these women were scarce, however. By 1850, the population of California was almost 93 percent male. In the mining regions, the percentage of men rose to 97.

Living in a nearly all-male world was shocking for many miners. For one thing, they had to perform domestic labor for the first time in their lives. Previously, they had always relied on their mothers, wives, sisters, and daughters to handle routine household tasks, such as cooking, cleaning, and doing laundry. In California, they might occasionally buy a meal at a boardinghouse or hire a Chinese man to clean their clothing, but these services were expensive. Out of necessity, men had to learn to perform these chores for themselves.

As a result, many men developed a new respect for what they called "women's work." One miner from Kentucky admitted as much in a letter to his sister: "I have always been enclined to deride the vocation of ladies until now but must confess it by far the more irksome I have tried & by way of taking lessons in sewing have often examined your stitches in my work bag."[6]

With few women around, unmarried miners became anxious about their future. In letters to their mothers and sisters, they often worried that, as one year in the mines turned into two or three, they were missing out on their chance ever to find

Living alone with little money forced miners to wash their own clothes, cook their own meals, and clean their own lodgings—responsibilities usually relegated to women. Even successful miners would often pine for their spouses, as depicted in this cartoon.

a wife. A bachelor named J.C. Colbreath put his fear into a letter home: "Society will be greatly changed when I return I am afraid few famliar faces will greet me the Girls will all be married."[7]

KEEPING IN TOUCH

Many men relied on letters to feel closer to the women in their lives. Not surprisingly, receiving a letter from home was often a cause for celebration. As one miner from Wisconsin wrote to his parents, "If you could have seen us when we received our letters, you would have laughed, perhaps called us fools—such hoorahing, jumping, yelling, and screaming."[8]

Letters also often led to soul-searching. A storekeeper named William Perkins explained his own bittersweet reaction to mail delivery: "There is a charm, a witchcraft in a letter from Home . . . , a man is transported at once in spirit to the scenes he has left behind. . . . My letters generally make me feel a little ashamed of finding myself in this country, leading a kind of savage life merely for the accumulation of gold."[9]

Of course, miners had a valid reason to fear a newly arrived letter. Often, they contained unwelcome news. At a time when epidemics were common, a letter from home might announce the unexpected death of parent or even of a child.

A NEW WORLD BACK HOME

When miners arrived in California, they found themselves in a strange society that they had to struggle to understand. The social upheaval in the communities they left was almost as jarring, however. Often, the most difficult adjustment for miners' wives was taking on the traditionally male role of breadwinner. Just as their husbands had to learn to perform women's work, many women had to work outside the house for the first time.

For some, it was a nerve-wracking experience. They were often stuck trying to run a family business that was already failing. Frequently, men left for California because their businesses were mired in debt, and from the moment they headed west, their wives found themselves dealing with creditors while desperately trying to keep the business afloat. Many women's letters to California complained of the financial straits the husbands had left them in. Others railed about their husbands' failures to make good on their promises of quick gold strikes.

Even a woman's business success could lead to tension in a marriage. Illinois farmer Jonathan Heywood praised his wife's hard work in keeping the family farm going, but he added, "I am almost afraid you are making more improvements and more money on the farm than I could if I were there."[10] It seems, the notion that his wife was doing his job better than he could was a source of anxiety for Heywood.

CIVILIZING CALIFORNIA

Lonely and exhausted by trying to make ends meet without their husbands' help, some wives wanted to come to California. In a heart-wrenching letter to her husband, Maria Tuttle desperately made her case: "Oh Charles I wish you would send for me or come after me. How much I would like to go to California. My ambition does not in the least abate. I would be willing to share with you almost any difficulties I could become independent and live in easy but plain circumstances."[11]

Miners generally did not want their wives to join them, however. Some were concerned about their wives' health and safety in taking the long trip to California. Others, considering the high cost of living in California, did not want to be responsible for another mouth to feed. Still others, including men in happy marriages, were not yet willing to give up the sense of independence that California gave them.

Even as they dissuaded their wives from coming, men of the Gold Rush almost universally bemoaned California's lack of women. The all-male world was new and exciting, giving many men an enticing escape from convention that they had never felt before and would never feel again. But they also sensed that there was something peculiar about this California, as though it were trapped in a state of perpetual adolescence. Like most men in nineteenth-century America, they saw women as a civilizing force. Only with a population of women, they believed, would California ever have a chance to grow up.

Mining
the Miners

The men who came to California during the Gold Rush all had one dream—to make a fortune in gold. Once they arrived in the gold fields, however, some became disillusioned. Mining, it turned out, was a difficult and physically taxing profession, and, unlike what many men believed when they left home, finding gold was far from a sure thing. As time went on, miners increasingly referred to mining as a lottery, a game that rewarded only a lucky few.

They also discovered that mining was not the only way to make money in California. In fact, as the rush wore on, there seemed to be more and more opportunities for enterprising men tired of the risk and wear of life in the mines. With a little hard work, a man could earn a good living in the growing California economy. If that man had some business savvy, he might become as rich as even the luckiest miner.

SETTING UP SHOP

Many of the first businesses established in Gold-Rush California involved mining the miners—that is, offering goods and services to miners in exchange for gold. Initially, the miners' needs were limited. Before heading to the mines, they went shopping in San Francisco, Sacramento, or Stockton for clothing, tools, and food staples such as flour and preserved meat.

It was simple to start a store. All a man had to do was erect a tent and display his wares on makeshift wooden benches. What was not so easy was figuring out what miners needed most at any given time. Especially in the rush's early years, the flow of goods into San Francisco was unpredictable. One week, a scarcity of boots would drive their price sky high. The next week, a few ships full of boots might sail into the bay, causing a glut of the product and driving down its price. Only a clever and attentive shopkeeper could do well, given the rapid fluctuations in the market.

TRANSPORTATION TO THE MINES

Early entrepreneurs immediately spotted another way to make money quickly. Just as much as miners needed food and supplies, they also had to find a way to carry them to the mines. By 1849, all sorts of transportation companies were already in operation.

Shipping companies sold tickets on steamships that took miners from San Francisco to either Sacramento or Stockton. For traveling the rivers of California, shipmakers in New York and Boston created new types of ships, which were both smaller and faster. The ships were broken down into parts and sent from these eastern cities in the storage hulks of larger vessels. As more and more ships reached San Francisco, shipping companies began to offer miners daily service. With competition, the ships themselves became more lush and eventually earned the nickname "floating palaces."

From Sacramento and Stockton, cargo companies carried men and goods to the mining camps. At first, simple wooden freight wagons made the rugged journey over dirt roads. After 1851, these were replaced by stagecoaches, which made the trip much faster and more comfortable.

DELIVERING THE MAIL

Other smart businessmen took advantage of the fact that northern California had virtually no government institutions. They offered for-pay services that were provided for free by the government in other parts of the United States. The most lucrative was mail delivery.

Always eager to hear from friends and family back home, miners were desperate to receive letters. In 1849, there was only one postal agent working in San Francisco. In November of that year, three months' worth of mail addressed to the city—about 45,000 letters—arrived at the post office on the same day. Even with four employees working with the agent, the office shut down for three days just to sort them. All the while, angry miners pounded on the office's door, threatening to riot. When the office finally reopened, miners had to wait in line for six hours to find out if they had any mail.

Sensing a great business opportunity, some men quit the mines and started to deliver mail. Typically, a miner would pay a mail delivery service one or two dollars to fetch his mail in the city and hand deliver it to him in his mining camp. A mail deliverer might have as many as 2,000 clients, bringing him a hefty profit.

Some mail services expanded into gold delivery. They contracted with miners to carry their gold to San Francisco and deposit it in a bank there. The service was valuable to miners who were fearful that thieves in the camps might get their hands on their take. For peace of mind, they were more than happy to pay a 5 percent fee for this service.

POST OFFICE, SAN FRANCISCO, CALIFORNIA.
A FAITHFUL REPRESENTATION OF THE CROWDS DAILY APPLYING AT THAT OFFICE FOR LETTERS AND NEWSPAPERS.

Homesick miners overwhelmed the San Francisco Post Office *(above)* as letters poured in from all over the United States. As gold mining became more competitive with the constant influx of new miners, some men quit their claims to make a fortune in providing services, such as mail delivery, to other miners.

SERVING MINERS

Miners generally hated wasting time on everyday chores that could be better spent mining or relaxing. Many entrepreneurs saw that they could make a quick buck by opening a restaurant that would relieve tired miners of their cooking duties. One restaurant catered to 12 to 20 boarders who each paid $16 per week. With the provisions needed to feed each man costing only $5 a week, the proprietor soon became wealthy.

A man named Solomon Gorgas wrote home about venturing into the restaurant business. Perhaps to justify abandoning mining, he emphasized his pride in the service he was provid-ing: "You may imagine me, most of the time, busily engaged waiting on my customers, whom I serve with pies & cakes & beer & brandy & everything that is good to eat & to drink—all prepared by our own hands with the assistance of a cook, & all nice and clean of course."[1]

Professionals also found ways to prosper in the Gold Rush. There were few doctors and dentists in the gold region, so they could charge exorbitant fees for their services. A miner with a raging fever or an aching tooth might grumble about the cost, but he had little choice but to pay it if he wanted to get well enough to return to the mines. A shortage of lawyers hiked up fees to settle legal disputes. A lawyer named William Dainger-field made $3,300 during his first 10 days in California.

Miners generally had a poor opinion of lawyers and doc-tors. They considered these professionals to be lazy and greedy, preying on men who were not afraid of a hard day of physical labor. Even more hated, though, were money lenders. Miners sometimes ran out of money before they could buy a claim or even get out to the mines. They had little choice but to borrow money from businessmen with cash to lend. Lending money could be astoundingly profitable. In 1849, lenders might charge as much as 60 percent interest in a month. As a result, in just two months, a lender could double his wealth. This business was risky, though: Plenty of men skipped out on their debts, leaving lenders high and dry.

GAMBLING HALLS

Miners also considered owners of gambling halls to be leeches, out to steal their hard-earned money. That did not stop men from patronizing their businesses, however. Many gamblers were ex-miners who knew firsthand how, on Sunday, a bored man might be persuaded to game away his week's take.

In the towns of the mining region, gambling houses were little more than crude tents. Still, they were appealing to men looking for a place to relax and socialize, as a miner named John Eagle explained: "Some go to gamble, some to drink, some to hunt up old acquaintances, some to hear the music. These are the only public places we have, and hard places they are, but all classes can be seen there occasionally."[2]

In San Francisco, gambling halls were much more elaborate. Chandeliers hung from their ceilings, and risqué paintings of female nudes adorned their walls. While gaming, men could enjoy the finest liquor or smoke the best cigars available. For many men, though, the gambling halls' greatest appeal was scantily dressed gambling-hall girls, who chatted and flirted with the patrons. Henry Packer wrote to his wife, perhaps in too much detail, of one gambling-hall women's appeal: "By Heaven a woman stands in the door—she is richly dressed. In her ears and on her fingers are massive gold rings displayed around her neck is a chain of the same. Glossy curls play over her full neck and shoulders. On her countenance plays a smile that would bewitch if not be guile a miniester."[3]

A FORTUNE IN FARMING

Northern California was blessed with plenty of fertile land. With miners tired of paying top dollar for imported food, it is not surprising that some took up farming. Many were already skilled farmers. Also, just about anyone could start a farm, even if he had little money in hand. No one formally owned the farmland, so a farmer could just mark out a plot and start working it.

In 1850, John Horner did just that. With a partner, he claimed 130 acres, on which they planted potatoes, onions, tomatoes, and cabbages. That year alone, they grossed $150,000 from the sale of their vegetables. As Horner quite rightly noted, "We flourished perhaps as no farmers ever flourished before in America, in so short a time."[4]

Another farmer named George C. Briggs struck it big in 1851 with a crop of watermelons. With $5,000 of profits in his pocket, he returned to Ohio and persuaded his wife to start a new life with him in California. Briggs imported seeds of fruit trees from the East and established a huge orchard. His success showed that California had a perfect climate for growing fruit.

Still, many miners, even those willing to give up the gold fields, were unenthusiastic about becoming farmers. They had traveled to California to get away from the farming life, which required just as much hard work as mining but provided none of the thrill of potentially making a big pile of money. Also, working a farm required a commitment to stay in one place

LUZENA WILSON
(c 1820–1902)

Woman of the West

As a woman, Luzena Wilson was an oddity among the overlanders who traveled to California in 1849. That spring, she set out from Missouri for the West with her husband and her two young boys.

The life she carved out in California was also unconventional. As her family neared Sacramento, a man asked if he could buy one of her homemade biscuits. He offered her five dollars. Wilson was dumbstruck by the astronomical offer, but before she could speak, he upped his offer to ten dollars. Wilson knew then that her domestic skills could be worth a small fortune in this strange land.

Her family settled in Sacramento and invested in a small hotel, where Wilson cooked for the guests. The business thrived until in late December, when a massive flood destroyed the hotel. The family then moved to the mining camp of Nevada City. There, Wilson established a new hotel that she called El Dorado. As she later explained, and perhaps even to make a permanent home in California. For miners who had expected to make a quick strike and then head back home, that commitment was difficult to make.

INVESTING IN THE FUTURE

Some of the most successful entrepreneurs were men who believed in the future of California. Many people assumed that, when the gold was gone, California would also fade away. These entrepreneurs, however, thought that California would continue to thrive and were willing to bet their fortunes on it.

"I bought two boards from a precious pile belonging to a man who was building the second wooden house in town. With my own hands I chopped stakes, drove them into the ground, and set up my table. . . . When my husband came back at night he found . . . twenty miniers eating at my table."[*] The El Dorado did good business until it burned to the ground in a fire nine months later.

Once again the Wilsons had to start over from scratch. They started a third hotel and a family farm in an area that became known as Vacaville. Mason, her husband, eventually abandoned the family, but Luzena stayed on. In time, she became one of Vacaville's leading citizens, prospering by selling real estate in the town she helped found. A successful businesswoman who had survived a rollercoaster of booms and busts, Luzena Wilson died in San Francisco in 1902 at the age of 83.

---

[*]Jo Ann Levy, *They Saw the Elephant: Women in the California Gold Rush.* Norman: University of Oklahoma Press, 1992.

One such entrepreneur was Sam Brannan. With the earnings from his stores, he began to invest in real estate. He focused on Sacramento, where he bought more than 500 prime lots. His investments eventually made him California's first millionaire.

Thomas Larkin was another successful real estate mogul. Even before gold was discovered, he was buying lots in San Francisco. In late 1849, Larkin sold nine of them for a stunning profit. They fetched $300,000 but had cost him a mere $1000.

Real estate investment was not without its risks, however. Between 1849 and 1852, San Francisco suffered through a series of massive fires. In the same period, Sacramento was destroyed not just by fire but also by severe flooding. With every disaster, building and business owners throughout these cities saw their fortunes destroyed in an instant. Some gave up and went home, but most shrugged off thoughts of their misfortunes and immediately focused on rebuilding what they had lost. One miner from France marveled at the cities' entrepreneurs and their relentless pursuit of success. He wrote, "One calamity more or less seems to make no difference to these Californians."[5]

Taking Control

At the beginning of the Gold Rush, no one cared that California had no government in place. In fact, miners were happy that it did not. They did not have to worry about any government authority interfering with their mining or claiming a right to a portion of their gold.

Californians soon recognized, though, that as San Francisco and the gold fields expanded, they needed to establish a government—and the sooner the better. In some instances, they had been well-served by smart entrepreneurs who had stepped in to offer services usually provided by governmental institutions. More often, however, for-profit companies took undue advantage. Private firefighters, for example, would negotiate prices while a man's home or business burned, jacking up the cost as the fire spread.

Californians were also eager for a real police force and court system. With the rough code of justice in the mines, everyone was anxious living in an essentially lawless society. Official courts were desperately needed to settle disputes over claims and property. In addition, many Americans coveted the vast land holdings of Californio ranching families. They wanted an official American-run institution in which they could challenge the ranchers' rights to this land.

GOVERNING CALIFORNIA

As tens of thousands of men headed to California in early 1849, many Americans assumed that the U.S. government would be eager to exert control over the gold region. They were stunned when Congress adjourned that March without making any firm decisions about what to do with California. The problem was the issue of slavery. The South wanted slavery legal in California, whereas the North wanted it outlawed. Unable to make a quick decision, Congress ignored the California question altogether.

When the news reached California, many prominent people there were annoyed. True to their can-do spirit, though, they decided to take matters into their own hands. On June 3, they issued a call for the election of delegates to a constitutional convention in Monterey.

In September, 48 delegates arrived in the town. They held meetings in Colton Hall, the only building in Monterey large enough to hold them all. Monterey was such a backwater that it did not even have enough hotel rooms for all the delegates; some brought their own bedrolls and spent their nights sleeping outside under the stars. Thomas Larkin, Monterey's wealthiest citizen, did what he could to make the delegates' stay comfortable: He invited a different delegate to his home everyday for lunch and dinner, just to make sure that each occasionally had a good meal.

THE CONSTITUTIONAL CONVENTION

The delegates agreed on one thing right off the bat. They did not want California to be an American territory. Territorial status was generally afforded to areas that eventually would become states but first needed to build up their populations. With more and more people flooding into California every month, it made sense to skip the territorial stage and move directly to statehood.

Unlike Congress, the delegates also had little trouble agreeing about slavery in California. They determined that it should be illegal in the state. Their decision was not based on morality but instead on economics. Early in the Gold Rush, some Southerners brought slaves to mine for them, but most miners condemned the practice, feeling that it gave slave owners an unfair advantage. Forbidding slavery in California merely formalized a social code that was already in place.

The delegates also decided to give women more rights than they enjoyed in most other states. For instance, they gave women a good deal of control over the assets they brought into a marriage. Again, the delegates were motivated less by a sense of fairness than by a practical concern. They wanted to do what they could to attract women to settle in California, knowing that if the state were to grow and prosper it would need a more gender-balanced population.

"CALIFORNIA IS A STATE"

After six weeks, the delegates had drafted a constitution. They printed 1,000 copies in English and 250 in Spanish and circulated them throughout California. On November 13, 1849, California held its first election. The turnout was low, but voters overwhelmingly approved the new constitution. They also elected a governor, a legislature, and two representatives to Congress.

The new state government sent the constitution to Washington, D.C., for approval. The government did not wait to hear back before holding its first legislative session, however.

In early 1850, the California legislature met for four months. In keeping with the unruly society of the era, the session was known as the "legislature of a thousand drinks" because of the large amount of liquor the lawmakers consumed. Still, they passed nearly 150 statutes, including the notorious Foreign Miners' Tax.

The legislature also established 27 counties. The counties were concentrated in the mining region, giving northern California much more power than southern California. Northerners immediately tried to levy heavy taxes on southern landowners, especially targeting Californio ranchers.

On October 18, 1850, a steamship delivering mail sailed into San Francisco Bay. From it hung a giant banner that declared, "California Is a State." Congress had formally accepted California's constitution, allowing it to enter the union as the thirty-first state. In San Francisco, Californians immediately threw an impromptu party. After important citizens made speeches in Portsmouth Square, celebrants giddily shot their pistols in the air while fireworks exploded over the city.

Out in the mines, no one seemed particularly interested in California's political fortunes. Concentrating all their efforts on striking it rich, miners were largely indifferent to news of California's statehood. As one miner from Mississippi explained, "There is not one man in a hundred that cares a damn about it, one way or another. All they want is what gold they can get, and the state may go to hell, and they would vamoose for home."[1]

THE COMMITTEE OF VIGILANCE

Even after achieving statehood, the government did little to address the mass lawlessness in California. Most officials proved to be hopelessly corrupt, willing to turn a blind eye to any crime if the bribe was large enough. Between 1850 and 1853, there were an astounding 1,200 murders in San Francisco. During that time, only one murderer was convicted through the city's official legal system.

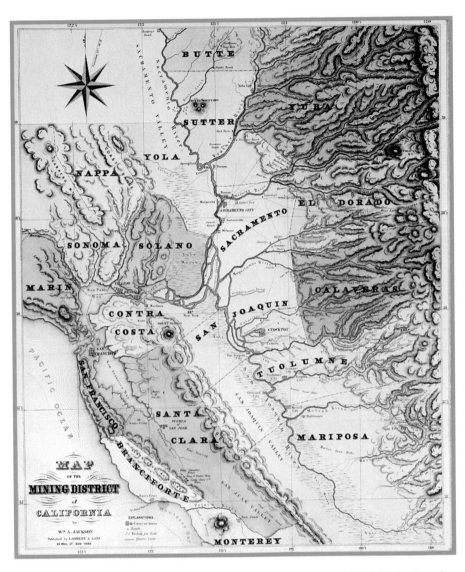

When California officially became a state, government officials declared there would be 27 counties. Most of the counties were in northern California, giving the mining region more political power than the agricultural-oriented southern portion of the state.

Taking matters in their own hands, vigilante groups emerged from time to time to wreak vengeance on suspected criminals.

(continues on page 82)

"TO HUNT [THEM] DOWN LIKE BEASTS"

During the Gold Rush, Americans treated the Indians of California with alarming brutality. They did not believe that these tribes had any rights to the lands that they had occupied for centuries. As a result, state officials made no effort to concentrate the Indians on reservations. Instead, they sought to exterminate California's Indian population by implicitly and sometimes explicitly promoting violence against them.

The following account of an Indian massacre appeared in the *Sacramento News* on March 6, 1853. Typical of such reports, the article suggested that the Indians started the violence by stealing from whites. In fact, when a theft occurred, non-Indians often used it as a justification to attack Indians who had nothing to do with the crime. The captive Indian children mentioned at the article's end were most likely enslaved:

The Indians have committed so many depredations in the North, of late, that the people are engaged against them, and are ready to knife them, shoot them, or inoculate them with small pox—all of which have been done.

Some time since, the Indians in Colusa county destroyed about some $5,000 worth of stock belonging to Messrs. Thomas & Toombe; since which time they have had two men employed, at $8.00 per month to hunt down and kill the Diggers [a derogatory term for California Indians], like other beasts of prey. On Friday, the 25th ult., one of these men, named John Breckenridge, was alone, and armed only with a bowie knife, when he met with four Indians and attacked them. They told him to leave, and commenced shooting arrows at him; but, undaunted, he

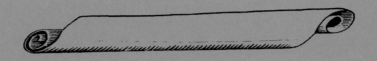

continued to advance, and succeeded in killing one, and taking one prisoner, while the other two escaped. He immediately proceed to Moon's Ranch, where the captured Indian was hung by the citizens.

On Friday, the 25th Feb., stock was stolen from Mr. Carter of Butte county, to the value of $3,000. . . . [A] party of twelve men [went] in search of the Indian depredators. . . . [O]ne detachment of the party discovered a half-breed by the name of Battedou, and took him prisoner. The man, fearing for his own life, agreed to show the cave where the Indians were concealed, if they would release him. . . .

Arriving there at early daylight on Tuesday morning, rocks were rolled into the cave, and the wretched inmates, rushing out for safety, met danger a thousand times more dreadful. The first one that made his appearance was shot by Capt. Geo Rose, and the others met the same fate from the rifles of the Americans. Altogether, there were thirteen killed; three chiefs of different rancherias, and three women. Three women and five children were spared; and it is but doing justice to say, that the women who were killed were placed in front of a sort of breast-work and killed either by accident or mistake. Capt. Rose took one child, Mr. Lattimer another, and the others were disposed of in the same charitable manner among the party.[*]

---

[*]Clifford E. Trafzer and Joel R. Hyer, eds., *"Exterminate Them": Written Accounts of the Murder, Rape, and Slavery of Native Americans During the California Gold Rush, 1848–1868.* East Lansing: Michigan State University Press, 1999.

(continued from page 79)

The most notorious was the Committee of Vigilance, which first emerged in 1851. The previous year, San Francisco had seen a rash of fires, possibly set by gangs that were intent on looting businesses as the city burned. Businessmen struck back by assembling the Committee of Vigilance, which was essentially a private army meant to punish the looters and intimidate anyone else who might want to threaten the business owners' livelihoods.

In 1856, businessmen revived the Committee of Vigilance when they began to worry that San Francisco's reputation for crime was discouraging investment in the city. For months, the committee staged a killing spree, murdering dozens of people that it branded criminals. The governor of California asked the U.S. government for help in stopping the committee, but, before the government could take action, the city's businessmen dissolved their army and held a parade to celebrate their illegal campaign against crime.

MINING WITH DAMS

In San Francisco, a city built on gold, it is hardly surprising that businessmen wield so much power. Large and powerful business concerns were also establishing much more control over the gold fields by the early 1850s. During this time, mining as an individual or a team enterprise declined. Instead, as gold became harder to find, it emerged as an industry run by well-funded companies. To make a fortune, miners now needed equipment and employed techniques that were far more complex and expensive than panning or washing dirt in a cradle.

The simplest of these new techniques was damming, which was first performed as early as 1849. To get full access to a riverbed and the gold-laden dirt within it, groups of miners would dam a river, diverting its water into a ditch some distance from the original bed.

Sometimes a dozen or more miners joined together to form a damming company, and the work took months of heavy labor. Just for timber and supplies during this period, a company could run up $10,000 worth of expenses before even washing a pail of dirt. To raise enough capital, companies often had to take on outside investors.

RISKY ENTERPRISES

In the gamble of mining, damming substantially upped the ante. A miner had to invest labor and money into a dam, with no guarantee that anything would come of it. Sometimes after completing a dam, a company might find that their claim was barren. Other times, a flash flood might wipe away a dam in minutes, leaving the company without a penny to show for all of their hard work and investment. A miner named Richard Cowley expressed the exasperation felt by many men who tried damming: "Daming Rivers does not pay. I have had a hand in making three dams on the river. I am certain I never will be one of the party to build the fourth one."[2]

By 1851, many miners had been overcome by "quartz mania." They believed that their future lay in quartz mining, which sought to free veins of gold embedded in great rocks made of quartz. Quartz mining took even more capital than damming. It required heavy machinery to pound the quartz into dirt that miners could then wash in search of gold. The machines could cost as much as $100,000, so outside investment was a necessity.

Miners and investors made heady by quartz mania soon came back down to earth: Quartz mining proved to be a disappointment. During the 1850s, only one percent of the gold found in California was unearthed using this technique.

HYDRAULIC MINING

Much more effective than quartz mining was hydraulic mining—that is, mining that made use of the power of water.

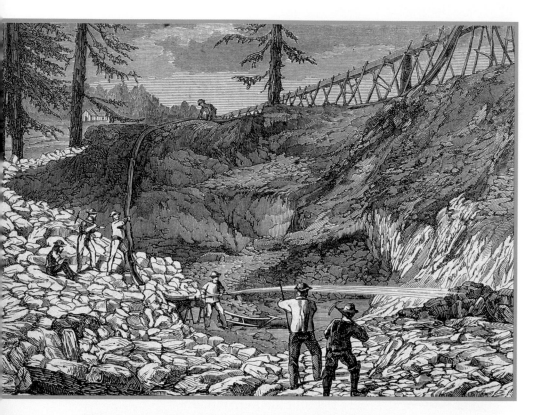

Bigger companies with investors and resources were able to pour money into new methods of finding gold, such as hydraulic mining *(above)*. Independent miners, however, could not compete with the efficiency of these large enterprises. Many miners had to give up their solitary work for employment with a mining company.

Through trial and error, miners found ways to divert river water into a hose, which could squirt out a stream at intense pressure. When aimed at a hillside, the pressured water could turn the solid rock into washable dirt. The *Sacramento Weekly Union* enthusiastically described this new mining method in July 1854: "Ten men who own a claim are enabled . . . by directing streams of water against the base of a high bank to cut away such an extent as to cause immense slides of earth which often bring with them large trees and heavy boulders."[3]

With the popularity of hydraulic mining, water became a valuable resource, and water companies arose to take advantage of the situation. They built dams and flumes to redirect river water to mining areas and then charged a steep price for use of this water by hydraulic mining firms.

Hydraulic mining allowed mining companies to find gold in less time and with less work than ever before. As the *Nevada Journal* explained in 1857, "Now water is used as the laboring agent and only men enough to keep the machinery properly directed are required. Thus banks of earth that would have kept a hundred men employed for months in their removal will now be removed by three or four men in two weeks."[4]

To successful investors, this meant big profits. To most miners, however, it meant that they had fewer opportunities than ever before. When the Gold Rush began, one miner could conceivably make a fortune working on his own. A decade later, with the labor-saving innovations of hydraulic mining, he could not even be sure of finding a job within a mining company that paid a decent wage.

The End of
the Rush

As the world of the Gold Rush was changing, one thing remained the same—the dream of a fortune in gold that compelled men to head off for California. Well into the 1850s, newcomers arrived determined to mine for riches. For them, the journey was far easier than it was for those who came in the first few seasons. The trip was cheaper, faster, and more predictable, and once in California, they also knew better what to expect. Later miners had read newspaper stories about the latest mining methods or letters from friends and family about the wonders of San Francisco and the challenges of the mining country.

Of course, the late arrivals had also heard plenty of sad tales from California—stories of hard-working miners who found no gold, of 49ers who lost a big strike in bad investments, of men so devastated by California that they gave themselves over to alcohol. They chose to ignore those tales; the idea of easy wealth was so exciting, they blocked out everything else. Despite all evidence to the contrary, these men believed that they would be the ones to beat the odds, the ones to succeed where so many others had failed.

"MINING IS LIKE AN OLD MAN"

It was virtually impossible for men who had already spent several seasons in California to be so naïve. With increased competition, especially from powerful companies, they could not pretend that their prospects in the mines were anything but dim and growing dimmer. As early as 1850, Richard Cowley expressed the kind of world-weariness that only became stronger the longer a miner stayed in the gold region: "Mining is not what it was when it was first discovered, men could make something handsome then, but it is in my opinion that mining is like an old man—it has seen its best days."[1]

Even if they were realistic about the present, many wizened miners felt nostalgic for California's "best days." They tended to blame their lack of success on timing. If only they had arrived sooner, they told themselves, everything would have been different. As one miner wrote forlornly, "Had I got here one year sooner I could have maid some thing but as it is I do not expect to make any thing worth while."[2]

As their spirits flagged, so did their bodies. One season in the mines exerted an enormous strain, as a mining team might dig and wash hundreds of buckets of dirt every day. The overuse of their back and leg muscles often led to injuries and sometimes to chronic pain. Poor sanitation spread disease, and a lack of fruits and vegetables often led to scurvy, an illness that caused miners' teeth to fall out. Days in the hot sun darkened and wrinkled their skin, and, overcome with stress and anxiety, many men watched their dark hair turn white. As a newspaper editor wrote in 1858, "Nowhere do young men look so old as in California."[3]

STAYING AND GOING

Considering their physical and mental exhaustion, why did many seasoned miners stay in California? For some, the reason was purely monetary. They may have invested in a dam, a flume, or some other scheme and were obliged to wait and see whether it would yield a profit. If they left too early, they might also leave behind a good return on their investment.

Others remembered all too well the grandiose promises that they had made when they set out on their great adventure. They had worked hard to persuade their families that they were doing the right thing, assuring their relatives that they would come home rich. The idea of returning with nothing was so horrible that, against their better judgment, these miners headed back to the mines season after season just to put off that awful day.

Often, families made it clear that they did not want their relatives in California to come home until they had made their strike. Women, children, and parents had frequently made enormous sacrifices to send their loved ones to the gold fields. Like the miners themselves, they were not eager to admit that it had all been for nothing.

Even if a man had had some success, he might find it hard to face his family. As men set off for California, especially in the Gold Rush's early seasons, news reports often emphasized that, if a man worked hard, he was sure to do well. Used to a rural way of life, where hard work usually did yield a decent living, this equation made sense. As miners soon learned, however, this was not true in California, where winning and losing were determined by dumb luck more than anything else.

Explaining this to the folks back home was difficult. Men knew that, if they came home with less gold than expected, they could face harsh judgment from their communities. Their friends and family might assume that they were lazy in the mines or, worse, that an indulgence in alcohol or gambling was the reason for their less-than-stellar take. As one miner explained, "I dislike the idea very much of returning without making any thing . . . besides I know that a good deal would be said about me as every person in the states think that no person that is industrious can come out here without making a fortune."[4] Some men were willing to chance it in California for season after season rather than face public condemnation, however undeserved.

A WORLD WITHOUT FAILURE

While some stayed in California to avoid going home, others remained because they wanted to. For failed miners, California offered a comfort that nowhere else in the states could. Everywhere else in America, economic failure was a badge of shame. In California, it barely had a stigma at all.

Just about everyone in California had failed at something, but there, one failure often meant the beginning of a success in another field. A failed miner might become a wealthy shopkeeper. A restaurant owner could lose his business to fire only to find real riches in mail delivery. A lawyer who had trouble finding clients might reinvent himself as a traveling circus performer. Such sudden reversals would baffle most Americans, but in California they were almost routine.

Miners embraced California for other reasons, as well. With its constant change and growth, California offered many different ways for young men to make a livelihood. Back home, they had few, if any, prospects for earning a good living. Rather than return home and work as low-paid laborers, they opted to stay in California to see what kind of lives they could carve out there. One miner was particularly honest about his lack of interest in his old way of life: "I feel bad sometimes when I think of home and the comfort I am deprived of by being away. Then again, come to think of how dull it is at home, I do not want to be there."[5]

Many miners also grew to enjoy California life. Its beautiful landscapes and pleasant weather made many men want to settle down there. Its free-wheeling society was attractive as well. As one man explained, "The independence and liberality here and the excitement attending the rapid march of this country make one feel insignificant and sad at the prospect of returning to the old beaten path at home."[6]

The men who came to California had often felt constrained by traditional obligations to their family members and to their communities. In fact, many headed to the gold fields just to escape an overbearing parent or a failing marriage. Even if wealth had eluded them, they embraced the freedom they felt in California and were determined to stay at any cost. Some completely abandoned their old lives, adopting new names and cutting off all ties with their relatives. California allowed these men literally to begin their lives anew.

RUMORS OF NEW FINDS

By the late 1850s, most miners had given up on their dreams of gold wealth. They might still work in California's mines, but only as employees for mining companies, working for wages with no hope of striking it rich. For nearly everyone, mining had lost its exoticism and drama—it had become just another type of wage work.

Even faced with these realities, some still longed to recapture the thrill of the early days of the Gold Rush. Like addicts, they responded to every rumor of a new and promising gold strike, wherever it was. In the spring of 1855, there were whispers that huge amounts of gold had been found along the Kern River. Five thousand hopeful miners rushed there, only to find that the reports of gold were grossly exaggerated.

The Fraser River rush of 1858 was even more disappointing. Throughout the spring and summer, nearly 25,000 Californians headed north to the Fraser in British Columbia, Canada, in hopes at last of making that one big score. The rumors were at least somewhat correct. There was some gold, but it was difficult to mine during the region's relentless rain.

Longing for the excitement and opportunities that accompanied the Gold Rush when it first began, failed miners would quickly relocate to regions rumored to have gold. When they arrived at some of these places such as the Kern River region *(above),* **they discovered these rumors were greatly exaggerated.**

The gold in British Columbia was not up for grabs, anyway: The governor of the province declared that all miners had to buy a license from the government. He also tried to enforce rules of conduct to keep the miners from becoming too rowdy. A few Californians found some gold, but with the intrusions of the government in the mining region, none of them was able to recreate the no-holds-barred excitement of the early days of the California rush.

(continues on page 94)

THE DAYS OF "FORTY NINE"

Throughout the Gold Rush, miners found comfort and joy in singing songs about their experiences. Those who traveled overland sang songs while relaxing at night. A few of those songs—such as "Oh, Susanna" and "Sweet Betsy from Pike"—still rank among the best-loved American folk songs. In California, men also sang when gathered around campfires in the gold fields or in saloons in towns and cities. The lyrics of the songs told ribald and humorous stories, often of failed miners and their struggles.

In later decades, former miners also used song to celebrate their Gold Rush experience. Many of these songs lapsed into sentimentality, depicting a romantic era of ever-loyal friends that never really existed. One of the most popular told of the sweet "days of old and the days of gold and the days of Forty Nine." Below is an excerpt, as recorded in 1931.

> We are gazing now on old Tom Moore,
> A relic of bygone days;
> 'Tis a bummer, too, they call me now,
> But what care I for praise?
> It's oft, says I, for the days gone by,
> It's oft do I repine,
> For the days of old when we dug out the gold
> In those days of Forty Nine.
>
> My comrades they all loved me well,
> The jolly saucy crew;
> A few hard cases, I will admit

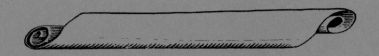

Though they were brave and true.
Whatever the pinch, they ne'er would flinch,
They never would fret nor whine,
Like good old brick they stood the kicks
In the days of Forty Nine. . . .

There was New York Jake, the butcher boy,
Who was fond of getting tight.
And every time he got on a spree
He was spoiling for a fight.
One night Jake rampaged against a knife
In the hands of old Bob Sine,
And over Jake they held a wake
In the days of Forty Nine. . . .

Of all the comrades that I've had
There's none that's left to boast,
And I am left alone in my misery
Like some poor wandering ghost.
And as I pass from town to town,
They call me the rambling sign,
Since the days of old and the days of gold,
And the days of Forty Nine.[*]

[*]The Days of Forty Nine. California Gold: Northern California Folk Music from the Thirties. Available online. URL: http://memory.loc.gov/cgi-bin/query/r?ammem/cowell:@FIELD(SOURCE+@band(afccc+@1(dysof))): @@@REF.

(continued from page 91)

ROMANTICIZING THE RUSH

Although those days were gone, memories of them stayed with the hundreds of thousands of Americans who had participated in the Gold Rush. As time passed, however, those memories began to change. Many men forgot about the physically painful labor, the crippling homesickness, and the brutal violence of the mining camps. They instead chose to remember the delight of making a gold find and the camaraderie they felt with their partners.

This romanticized version of the Gold Rush served many men well. Even if they failed to find treasure, they could feel that their experiences in California were worthwhile. The rush era not only provided them with the greatest adventure of their lives, but it also allowed them to take part in a great moment for the nation. This notion that the Gold Rush was a grand display of the grit and determination of the American people was especially pleasing in the years after the Civil War (1861–1865). After that national crisis, people cast a golden glow of nostalgia over California's early days, remembering it as a time when Americans banded together in a shared struggle for a rich reward.

Some former miners recalled the Gold Rush years with private celebrations. A man named William Swain hosted a formal dinner for his family each year to commemorate the day he returned from California. In the course of the festivities, his wife, Sabrina, always toasted William as "her Forty-Niner."[7]

Others formed societies to celebrate their gold mining days. These societies often held annual galas. After speeches about their glory days out West, aging men would sing maudlin songs about their youthful adventures.

FIFTY YEARS LATER

The grandest celebration of all occurred in California on January 24, 1898—the fiftieth anniversary of James Marshall's discovery of gold in the American River. In towns and cities throughout the state, Californians marched in parades and listened to their leading citizens deliver speeches about that great and defining moment in their state's history. Delegations of miners, now old men, gathered in San Francisco, where they were treated like celebrities.

Among those who returned was Azariah Smith. Fifty years before, at age 19, he had been one of a handful of men to hear of the gold discovery from Marshall himself. That distinction made Smith an object of fascination to the press and the public.

During his visit, Smith sat down with a reporter from the *San Francisco Examiner*. Almost sounding apologetic, Smith explained that the "news that glistening gold was all around did not make me as enthusiastic as it might have had."[8] Recalling how he left California just as the Gold Rush began, Smith noted, "I was home-sick as well as physically sick. I wanted to see my mother and did not care whether there was gold in the locality or not."[9]

To many readers, that might have sounded like regret. If only Smith had summoned the strength to ignore his physical exhaustion and homesickness, he could have been an actor in the greatest drama in the history of California, if not the history of the United States.

With the next question, though, Smith set the record straight. The reporter asked the 69-year-old if he ever wished he had stayed in California. Soberly, Smith replied, "If I'd stayed there I would have been under the ground in a short time."[10] Unaffected by the hoopla around him, Smith saw clearly that the secret to his long and happy life lay not in embracing the quest for gold but in running away from it.

Legacy of a Great Adventure

The people affected directly by the Gold Rush knew that they were living in special age. As soon as Americans began to head out for the gold fields, thousands started to collect their thoughts and feelings in letters and diaries. They saw themselves as part of a great epic and wanted to be sure that there were records of their roles in this grand story. As a result, the Gold Rush is perhaps the most widely documented event in American history.

The men and women of the Gold Rush tried their best to analyze their times and write about how it changed their friends, communities, and themselves. In many ways, though, they were too close to the era to see its long-term impact on the United States. Aside from the Civil War, the Gold Rush was the most significant event in nineteenth-century America. Its influence might have been even greater, stretching over many decades and affecting the way Americans live in the present and will likely live in the future.

HEADING WEST

One of the most lasting consequences of the Gold Rush was the massive migration west. Before the rush, most Americans did not venture far from their own communities. Few would ever have considered moving thousands of miles away from their families and friends to an unfamiliar land about which they knew almost nothing. The lure of California gold, however, made long-distance travel commonplace.

This comfort with overland treks and sea voyages did not only bring easterners to California, it also encouraged Americans to settle other regions in the West. In this way, the Gold Rush accelerated the speed of western settlement and thus of the Americanization of the lands that the United States acquired through the Mexican-American War.

By the late 1850s, travel to California was far more comfortable than it had been at the beginning of the rush. Businessmen there realized, however, that to continue to thrive, California needed to be connected to the rest of the United States by rail. Boosters tried to convince officials in Washington to build a railroad stretching from the Atlantic seaboard to California's Pacific shore. Consumed by the Civil War, the federal government at that time did not have the money and attention to build the dreamed-of transcontinental railroad.

Fueled by Gold Rush wealth and ambition, a group of four Sacramento merchants, including Leland Stanford, decided to take matters into their own hands. They formed the Central Pacific Railroad with the goal of laying tracks from California eastward. In 1861, Stanford became governor of California and garnered the support of the state legislature. The project was funded largely by investors who had become wealthy in the rush's boom years.

As gold fever subsided and people began to settle permanently in California, prominent Californians lobbied the federal government to construct a railroad that would connect the state to the rest of the country. While the federal government rejected plans for a transcontinental railroad, investors soon provided the funds to begin construction. Crews of workers pitched their tents near work sites and built the first American transportation system that stretched from one coast to another.

On May 10, 1869, in Utah, the final spike was driven and the transcontinental railroad was complete. The railroad made Americans more mobile than ever and forever tied the East to the West.

MAKING A STATE

Possibly the most obvious result of the Gold Rush was the quick growth of California itself. If gold had not been found in California, it eventually would have become a state, but with the influx of gold seekers, the process was accelerated by many years, if not many decades.

The miners' arrival also created new towns and cities out of whole cloth. The most cosmopolitan city was of course San Francisco. Having transformed from a small village into a major urban area in just a few months, San Francisco remains one of America's most vibrant cities today.

The city's long history of diversity started in the Gold Rush period. As thousands of miners from around the world came to San Francisco, it became one of the most socially and racially diverse societies in the world. As a result, American miners were exposed to other peoples and cultures, which sometimes challenged old prejudices. When the miners went home, they shared their experiences with other people, leading even more Americans to reconsider their preconceived notions about foreigners.

For many of these foreign immigrants, discrimination turned their adventure in California bitter. For others, coming to the gold fields was a positive experience overall. America ultimately gave these foreigners and their descendants more economic opportunities, religious freedom, and political rights than they would have had in their homelands.

CALIFORNIOS AND INDIANS

Particularly in the north, the Gold Rush was a disaster for the Californio ranching families who had once held sway in California. Increasingly, American farmers squatted on their large ranches, knowing that California authorities would do nothing to stop them. With the gold-fueled economy, some ranchers found it easy to borrow large sums of money, only to lose their land holdings when they were unable to pay their debts. Over time, these families lost much of their land and most of their power in California's new Americanized society.

The people who were most adversely affected by the Gold Rush, however, were California's native inhabitants. Even before the gold discovery, the region's Indian tribes were suffering from disease, hunger, and the aftermath of years of abuse at the Spanish missions. During the rush, their plight became even more desperate. With their lands overrun by miners, they could no longer obtain food from their traditional hunting and gathering areas. As a result, many Indians starved to death.

The state of California also passed several barbaric anti-Indian laws in the early 1850s. These laws essentially allowed Americans to enslave Indian men, women, and children and also sanctioned the state-sponsored murder of California's Indians. The state spent millions on bounties to "Indian hunters," who could earn as much as five dollars for each severed Indian head they could produce. Not surprisingly, the Indian population dropped sharply during the rush years—from 150,000 before gold was found to 30,000 in 1870.

TRASHING THE LAND

Gold miners treated the California landscape with almost as much brutality as they treated the Indians. The gold region was covered with trash. Whatever the miners no longer needed, they just left on the ground to rot. To most, California was only a temporary home. Because they knew they would not be there for long, they carelessly polluted the environment without a second thought.

Miners were equally reckless about what their mining methods did to the land. The mercury they used to capture gold polluted both the air and water. Even now, many rivers in northern California are contaminated with high levels of mercury, exposure to which can cause nervous system damage.

Hydraulic mining was especially destructive to the environment. Pulverizing hillsides with pressurized streams of water, miners created billions of tons of sediment. Dumped into rivers, this dirt destroyed huge areas of rich farmland downstream.

A more positive legacy of hydraulic mining was its effect on California's agricultural industry. As miners needed more water, many became amateur engineers and, through experimentation, developed new and better ways to transport this increasingly valuable resource. When the rush wound down, Californians used what they had learned about hydraulics to bring water to fields and orchards, allowing agriculture to become a major part of the state's economy.

Entrepreneurs also decimated the region's forests. To fulfill the demand for timber, they lay waste to great stands of oaks, pines, and redwoods. In doing so, they destroyed the habitats of many animal species.

LAND OF CHANGE, LAND OF PROMISE

Some of the most significant consequences of the Gold Rush were psychological. This convulsive event forced Americans to think about the world and sometimes themselves in a new way. For better or for worse, many came away from the experience having abandoned old traditions and beliefs.

In early nineteenth-century America, unbridled greed was viewed as a sin. When news of the California gold find spread, however, many men could not contain their desire to get their hands on some of the riches being torn from the land. To their relatives, they might try to cloak their gold-lust in comforting language about how they were headed to California for the good of their families, but once in the gold fields, they barely bothered to hide their naked need for wealth. Over time, the experiences of these miners made expressions of greed far more acceptable in American society.

Before the Gold Rush, Americans held firm to the belief that wealth could come only from hard work. In California, though, miners came face to face with the reality that luck was more often the guiding force behind success. A lazy miner could make a strike; a hard-working one could end up with nothing. In the miners' world, how a fortune was earned seemed to lose its importance. Increasingly, this idea seeped into American culture. Today, lottery winners or daytraders who, by chance,

CALIFORNIA AND THE PURSUIT OF HAPPINESS

For 160 years, scholars have examined the Gold Rush, struggling to make sense of this strange and complex period. According to Kevin Starr, professor of history at the University of Southern California, the era has inspired a wide variety of theories as to its true meaning:

> Historians have interpreted the Gold Rush successively as a mid-Victorian epic of Anglo-Saxon progress, . . . a case study in American self-government, . . . a moral crisis, . . . a challenge to community building, . . . a technological triumph, . . . an outpouring of entrepreneurial self-actualization, . . . a case study in the persistent and shaping influence of American institutions, . . . a transformation of America itself, . . . and . . . a nightmare of violence, lynch law, racism, genocide, xenophobia, class and sexual conflict, and brutal degradation of the environment.[*]

In his book *The Age of Gold* (2002), author H.W. Brands concluded by tying the meaning of the Gold Rush to one of the first recognized rights of the American people—the pursuit of happiness as described in Thomas Jefferson's Declaration of Independence:

> America's enthronement of individualism magnified the impact of the gold discovery; the gold rushes to Canada and Siberia

make a killing in the stock market are rarely held in contempt for their easy money. Instead, they are envied for their luck and the wealth it has brought them.

The Gold Rush also changed Americans' concept of failure. In early America, failure was a considered a sign of laziness and immorality. Men in California, however, began to think

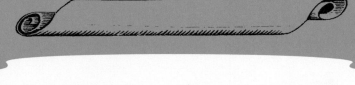

were more orderly than the rush to California. But they were also less history-shaping, partly because neither the Klondike nor Siberia was anyone's vision of paradise, but also because neither Canada nor Russia elevated the pursuit of happiness to the status of inalienable right, and when the gold of California promised a way to find happiness all at once, they couldn't resist.

And in this lay the ultimate meaning of the Gold Rush. The Gold Rush shaped history so profoundly because it harnessed the most basic of human desires, the desire for happiness. None of the gold-seekers went to California to build a new state, to force a resolution of the sectional conflict, to construct a trans-continental railroad, to reconstruct the American dream. They went to California to seek individual happiness. Some found it; some didn't. But the side effect of their pursuit—the cumulative outcome of their individual quests—was a transformation of American history. The men and women of the Gold Rush hoped to change their lives by going to California; in the bargain they changed their world.**

---

*Kevin Starr, *California: A History.* New York: Modern Library, 2005.
**H.W. Brands, *The Age of Gold: The California Gold Rush and the New American Dream.* New York: Doubleday, 2002.

On May 10, 1896, two trains, one from the East and one from the West, met in Utah for a ceremony to commemorate the completion of the transcontinental railroad. When the final spike was driven into the ground, it created the first mode of coast-to-coast transportation in the United States.

of failure as a part of life, the result of a bit of bad luck that could happen to anyone. With the shame removed from failure, Californians felt freer to try new things, especially as they saw the great rewards that could come from risk taking in business. In this way, the Gold Rush helped to foster a spirit of entrepreneurship in American culture.

One of the biggest ideas to come from the California Gold Rush was California itself. To the miners, California was, of course, a very real place whose sights, sounds, and smells many vividly recalled for their rest of their lives. At the same time, to them and to generations to come, it also seemed almost a mythical place of total freedom, of constant change, and of infinite promise.

Americans have always been an optimistic people. After the rush, California came to represent that very American trait. It is hardly a coincidence that Californians have long been known for their confident embrace of the new, as evidenced by Hollywood's movie studios and Silicon Valley's computer firms. In the America mind, California remains special. Even today, the Golden State is seen as a place where dreams come true and the future is born.

CHRONOLOGY

1542   Juan Rodríguez Cabrillo explores the coast of present-day California on behalf of Spain.

1769   Spanish priests establish the first mission in California.

1821   Mexico declares its independence from Spain, bringing California under Mexican control.

1839   Swiss entrepreneur Johann Sutter builds Sutter's Fort in northern California.

1846   **May 13** The United States goes to war with Mexico.

TIMELINE

January 24, 1848
James Marshall discovers gold at Sutter's Mill on the American River.

December 5, 1848
President James K. Polk confirms the gold find in his State of the Union address.

June 1849
The first miners traveling by the Cape Horn route arrive in California.

1848   1849

February 2, 1848
The Mexican-American War formally ends with an American victory; California becomes part of the United States.

April 1849
More than 30,000 people gather along towns on the Missouri River to prepare for the overland trek to California.

1848   **January 24** James Marshall discovers gold at Sutter's Mill on the American River.

February 2 The Mexican-American War formally ends with an American victory; California becomes part of the United States.

April 1 Merchant Sam Brannan announces the gold discovery in the streets of San Francisco.

August 19 The *New York Herald* reports the discovery of gold in California.

December 5 President James K. Polk confirms the gold find in his State of the Union address.

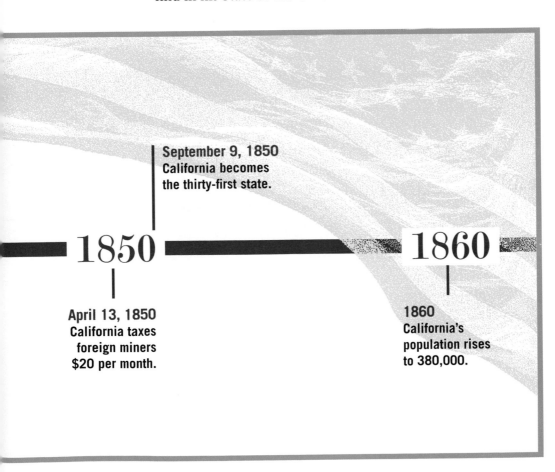

September 9, 1850
California becomes
the thirty-first state.

1850

1860

April 13, 1850
California taxes
foreign miners
$20 per month.

1860
California's
population rises
to 380,000.

1849   **February 17** The *California* arrives in San Francisco, marking the beginning of regular steamboat service to the city.

April More than 30,000 people gather along towns on the Missouri River to prepare for the overland trek to California.

June The first miners traveling by the Cape Horn route arrive in California.

November 13 Voters approve the California state constitution.

1850   **April 13** California taxes foreign miners $20 per month.

April 22 California's Act for the Government and Protection of Indians allows Americans to force Indians into servitude.

May–June Two massive fires burn more than 600 buildings in San Francisco.

September 9 California becomes the thirty-first state.

1851   **March 14** The tax on foreign miners is repealed.

Summer Quartz mining is first performed in California.

1853   Hydraulic mining is introduced in California.

1860   California's population rises to 380,000.

1998   Californians celebrate the one-hundred-fiftieth anniversary of the Gold Rush.

NOTES

CHAPTER 1

1. David L. Bigler, ed., *The Gold Discovery Journal of Azariah Smith*. Salt Lake City: University of Utah Press, 1990, p. 82.
2. Ibid., p. 105.
3. Ibid., p. 107.
4. Ibid., p. 108.
5. Ibid.
6. J.S. Holliday, *Rush for Riches: Gold Fever and the Making of California*. Berkeley: University of California Press, 1999, p. 56.
7. Bigler, *Gold Discovery Journal*, p. 110.
8. Ibid.
9. Holliday, *Rush for Riches*, p. 60.
10. Ibid., p. 61.
11. Bigler, *Gold Discovery Journal*, p. 113.
12. Ibid.

CHAPTER 2

1. Kevin Starr, *California: A History*. New York: Modern Library, 2005, p. 7.
2. Holliday, *Rush for Riches*, p. 19.

CHAPTER 3

1. Ibid., p. 61.
2. Ibid., p. 72.
3. Ibid., p. 64.
4. Ibid., p. 60.
5. Malcolm Rohrbough, *Days of Gold: The California Gold Rush and the American Nation*. Berkeley: University of California Press, 1997, p. 24.
6. Ibid.

CHAPTER 4

1. Holliday, *Rush for Riches*, p. 93.
2. Rohrbough, *Days of Gold*, p. 34.
3. Ibid., p. 37.
4. Ibid., p. 48.
5. Ibid., p. 47.
6. Ibid., p. 57.
7. Holliday, *Rush for Riches*, p. 98.
8. Rohrbough, *Days of Gold*, p. 63.
9. Holliday, *Rush for Riches*, p. 107.
10. Ibid.

CHAPTER 5

1. Rohrbough, *Days of Gold*, p. 66.
2. Ibid., p. 76.
3. Ibid., pp. 121–122.
4. Holliday, *Rush for Riches*, p. 123.
5. Ibid.

CHAPTER 6

1. Rohrbough, *Days of Gold*, p. 156.
2. Ibid., p. 72.
3. Ibid., p. 80.
4. Holliday, *Rush for Riches*, p. 128.
5. Ibid., p. 135.
6. Rohrbough, *Days of Gold*, p. 93.
7. Ibid., p. 101.
8. Holliday, *Rush for Riches*, p. 131.
9. Ibid.
10. Rohrbough, *Days of Gold*, p. 109.
11. Ibid., pp. 173–174.

CHAPTER 7

1. Ibid., p. 133.
2. Ibid., p. 148.
3. Ibid., p. 149.
4. Holliday, *Rush for Riches*, p. 194.
5. Ibid., p. 147.

CHAPTER 8

1. Ibid., p. 171.
2. Rohrbough, *Days of Gold*, p. 199.
3. Holliday, *Rush for Riches*, p. 210.
4. Ibid., p. 212.

CHAPTER 9

1. Rohrbough, *Days of Gold*, p. 187.
2. Ibid., p. 205.

3. Ibid., p. 192.
4. Ibid., p. 263.
5. Holliday, *Rush for Riches*, p. 159.
6. Ibid., p. 167.
7. Rohrbough, *Days of Gold*, p. 290.
8. Bigler, *Gold Discovery Journal*, p. 122.
9. Ibid.
10. Ibid., p. 124.

BIBLIOGRAPHY

Bigler, David L., ed. *The Gold Discovery Journal of Azariah Smith.* Salt Lake City: University of Utah Press, 1990.

Brands, H.W. *The Age of Gold: The California Gold Rush and the New American Dream.* New York: Doubleday, 2002.

Holliday, J.S. *Rush for Riches: Gold Fever and the Making of California.* Berkeley: University of California Press, 1999.

———. *The World Rushed In: The California Gold Rush Experience,* 2nd ed. Norman: University of Oklahoma Press, 2002.

Johnson, Susan Lee. *Roaring Camp: The Social World of the California Gold Rush.* New York: W. W. Norton, 2000.

Levy, Jo Ann. *They Saw the Elephant: Women in the California Gold Rush.* Norman: University of Oklahoma Press, 1992.

Roberts, Brian. *American Alchemy: The California Gold Rush and Middle-Class Culture.* Chapel Hill: University of North Carolina Press, 2002.

Rohrbough, Malcolm. *Days of Gold: The California Gold Rush and the American Nation.* Berkeley: University of California Press, 1997.

Trafzer, Clifford E., and Joel R. Hyer, eds. *"Exterminate Them": Written Accounts of the Murder, Rape, and Slavery of Native Americans During the California Gold Rush, 1848–1868.* East Lansing: Michigan State University Press, 1999.

FURTHER READING

BOOKS

Green, Carl R. *The California Trail to Gold in American History.* Berkeley Heights, N.J.: Enslow, 2000.

Holliday, J.S. *Rush for Riches: Gold Fever and the Making of California.* Berkeley: University of California Press, 1999.

Levy, Jo Ann. *They Saw the Elephant: Women in the California Gold Rush.* Norman: University of Oklahoma Press, 1992.

Lloyd, J.D., ed. *The Gold Rush.* San Diego: Greenhaven, 2002.

Trafzer, Clifford E., and Joel R. Hyer, eds. *"Exterminate Them": Written Accounts of the Murder, Rape, and Slavery of Native Americans During the California Gold Rush, 1848–1868.* East Lansing: Michigan State University Press, 1999.

WEB SITES

The American Experience: The Gold Rush
www.pbs.org/wgbh/amex/goldrush

"California as I Saw It": First-Person Narratives of California's Early Years, 1849–1900
www.memory.loc.gov/ammem/cbhtml/cbhome.html

"California as We Saw It": Exploring the California Gold Rush
www.library.ca.gov/goldrush

Gold Rush at *The Sacramento Bee*
www.calgoldrush.com

The Gold Rush: California Transformed. California Historical Society
www.californiahistory.net/goldFrame-2.htm

Gold Rush! California's Untold Stories, Oakland Museum of California

www.museumca.org/goldrush

San Francisco–Gold Rush, The Virtual Museum of the City of San Francisco

www.sfmuseum.org/hist1/index0.1.html#gold

Photo Credits

INDEX

ABOUT THE AUTHOR

LIZ SONNEBORN is a writer who lives in Brooklyn, New York. A graduate of Swarthmore College, she has written more than 60 books for children and adults, including *The American West, A to Z of American Indian Women, The Mexican-American War, The Mormon Trail,* and *Chronology of American Indian History.*

20284